Nathan D. Larson

ALEKSANDR SOLZHENITSYN AND THE MODERN RUSSO-JEWISH QUESTION

ibidem-Verlag
Stuttgart

Bibliographic information published by the Deutsche Nationalbibliothek
Die Deutsche Nationalbibliothek lists this publication in the Deutsche Nationalbibliografie; detailed bibliographic data are available in the Internet at http://dnb.d-nb.de.

Bibliografische Information der Deutschen Nationalbibliothek
Die Deutsche Nationalbibliothek verzeichnet diese Publikation in der Deutschen Nationalbibliografie; detaillierte bibliografische Daten sind im Internet über http://dnb.d-nb.de abrufbar.

Cover picture: *Midday* (painting of countryside near Moscow) by Ivan Shishkin, 1889. Source: http://commons.wikimedia.org/wiki/File:Shishkin_Polden_Okrestnosti_Moskvy.jpg. Public Domain

ISSN: 1614-3515

ISBN-13: 978-3-89821-483-4

Printed in the United States of America

Soviet and Post-Soviet Politics and Society (SPPS)

ISSN 1614-3515

Soviet and Post-Soviet Politics and Society (SPPS)

ISSN 1614-3515

Founded in 2004 and refereed since 2007, SPPS makes available affordable English-, German-, and Russian-language studies on the history of the countries of the former Soviet bloc from the late Tsarist period to today. It publishes between 5 and 20 volumes per year and focuses on issues in transitions to and from democracy such as economic crisis, identity formation, civil society development, and constitutional reform in CEE and the NIS. SPPS also aims to highlight so far understudied themes in East European studies such as right-wing radicalism, religious life, higher education, or human rights protection. The authors and titles of all previously published volumes are listed at the end of this book. For a full description of the series and reviews of its books, see www.ibidem-verlag.de/red/spps.

Editorial correspondence & manuscripts should be sent to: Dr. Andreas Umland, DAAD, German Embassy, vul. Bohdana Khmelnitskoho 25, UA-01901 Kyiv, Ukraine. e-mail: umland@stanfordalumni.org

Business correspondence & review copy requests should be sent to: ***ibidem*** Press, Leuschnerstr. 40, 30457 Hannover, Germany; tel.: +49 511 2622200; fax: +49 511 2622201; spps@ibidem.eu.

Authors, reviewers, referees, and editors for (as well as all other persons sympathetic to) SPPS are invited to join its networks at www.facebook.com/group.php?gid=52638198614 www.linkedin.com/groups?about=&gid=103012 www.xing.com/net/spps-ibidem-verlag/

Recent Volumes

114 Ivo Mijnssen
The Quest for an Ideal Youth in Putin's Russia I
Back to Our Future! History, Modernity and Patriotism according to *Nashi*, 2005-2012
With a foreword by Jeronim Perović
ISBN 978-3-8382-0368-3

115 Jussi Lassila
The Quest for an Ideal Youth in Putin's Russia II
The Search for Distinctive Conformism in the Political Communication of *Nashi*, 2005-2009
With a foreword by Kirill Postoutenko
ISBN 978-3-8382-0415-4

116 Valerio Trabandt
Neue Nachbarn, gute Nachbarschaft?
Die EU als internationaler Akteur am Beispiel ihrer Demokratieförderung in Belarus und der Ukraine 2004-2009
Mit einem Vorwort von Jutta Joachim
ISBN 978-3-8382-0437-6

117 Fabian Pfeiffer
Estlands Außen- und Sicherheitspolitik I
Der estnische Atlantizismus nach der wiedererlangten Unabhängigkeit 1991-2004
Mit einem Vorwort von Helmut Hubel
ISBN 978-3-8382-0127-6

118 Jana Podßuweit
Estlands Außen- und Sicherheitspolitik II
Handlungsoptionen eines Kleinstaates im Rahmen seiner EU-Mitgliedschaft (2004-2008)
Mit einem Vorwort von Helmut Hubel
ISBN 978-3-8382-0440-6

119 Karin Pointner
Estlands Außen- und Sicherheitspolitik III
Eine gedächtnispolitische Analyse estnischer Entwicklungskooperation 2006-2010
Mit einem Vorwort von Karin Liebhart
ISBN 978-3-8382-0435-2

120 Ruslana Vovk
Die Offenheit der ukrainischen Verfassung für das Völkerrecht und die europäische Integration
Mit einem Vorwort von Alexander Blankenagel
ISBN 978-3-8382-0481-9

121 Mykhaylo Banakh
Die Relevanz der Zivilgesellschaft bei den postkommunistischen Transformationsprozessen in mittel- und osteuropäischen Ländern
Das Beispiel der spät- und postsowjetischen Ukraine 1986-2009
Mit einem Vorwort von Gerhard Simon
ISBN 978-3-8382-0499-4

For Amber

List of Contents

Reproduced with kind permission from Dimitrii Sokolenko.
Location: http://www.pbase.com/dimitrisokolenko/image/33960668

I Introduction

The Jewish nation is thought by Aleksandr Solzhenitsyn to be the catalyst for all humanity.[1] This dynamic race has created an indelible mark in the history of the Russian Empire, the Soviet Union, and it will undoubtedly continue its courtship with post-Communist Russia. As we cast our minds back to the eighteenth-century partition of Eastern Poland, the annexation of which integrated roughly a million Jews into the Russian Empire, we peruse pages of history depicting the good and malevolent rendered by Russian and Jew alike to one another throughout generations. What has come to be known as the "Jewish Question"—the enigma of Jewish place in world history—is a contemporary reality in the eyes of many Russians and has assumed renewed color since the dissolution of the Soviet regime in 1991. Likewise, many Jews struggle to discover an identity amidst the new socio-political landscape of post-Communist Russia. This is one of the great love-hate relationships of history, neither race being unaffected.

As a part of his historical prose, Aleksandr Solzhenitsyn has written prolifically on the Jewish Question and has been both venerated as a prophet and castigated as an anti-Semite for so doing. The significant and at times reprehensible events surrounding prominent Jewish figures in Solzhenitsyn's novels have raised suspicious eyes ever since the writer's fame began escalating in the 1970s. Whilst the rich character development of the Jewish revolutionary Dmitri Bogrov in *August 1914* bears witness of the importance of the Jewish Question in Russian history, the attributes ascribed to Parvus from *Lenin in Zurich* certainly raise the question: is Solzhenitsyn anti-Semitic? Nevertheless, in Solzhenitsyn's canon there is an array of Jewish character types, some ignoble and others benevolent. Whether or not the writer's heart is free of prejudice, accusations of anti-Semitism have been profuse for decades and continue to the present day.

1 Viktor Loshak, „Raskalennyi vopros," *The Yonge Street Review* 149 <http://www.newcanada.com/149/vopros.htm> (as of 28 Jun. 2001).

Nowhere does the Jewish Question of Russia receive more attention than in response to the overtures of extreme right-wing nationalist groups. By virtue of Solzhenitsyn's advocacy of national rebirth he is deemed ethnically chauvinistic, even harboring prejudice towards Jews as many fanatical nationalists do. Notwithstanding, a close examination of the writer's taxonomy of nationalism reveals a patriot quite unlike radicals of inveterate xenophobic outlook.

In his years of imprisonment Aleksandr Solzhenitsyn came to believe that the struggle between good and evil cannot be resolved among parties, classes, or doctrines, but is waged within the individual human heart. This Tolstoian view and search for Christian ethics could not but seem heretical in the ideological environment of the Soviet Union. Ultimately, Solzhenitsyn emulates the great nineteenth-century Russian writers whose sense of literary truth rested on an absolute moral imperative. Out of this concern grew the exigency to discover the truth about Russo-Jewish historical relations.

Hoping to elucidate the volatile Russo-Jewish historical relationship and to exonerate himself of the anti-Semitic stigma, Solzhenitsyn dedicated nearly ten years to a two-tome work entitled *Двести лет вместе* (*Two Hundred Years Together*). This publication also prompted the appearance of a 1966 article, *Евреи в СССР и в будущей России* (*Jews in the USSR and in Future Russia*), attributed to Solzhenitsyn but condemned by the writer as a "falsification." Literary commentators have expressed bemusement at the time and ardor the writer has dedicated to this incendiary topic. Nevertheless, in the twilight of his life Solzhenitsyn has embarked on an historical work which traces the erratic relations between Jews and Russians in both the Imperial and Soviet eras.

Thus far, quite limited research has been undertaken of both the 1966 article and the two-volume series *Two Hundred Years Together*—most likely because neither has been entirely translated into English, only French. In response to such a need, this work seeks not to answer, but to illumine the present-day Jewish Question of Russia by analyzing these two newly-published works of Solzhenitsyn within the context of the writer's past work, his critics, Russian nationalism, and Russo-Jewish history.

As the analysis will show, Solzhenitsyn reflects his country's perpetual enigmatic nature. He is permeated by the metaphysical notion of the "Russian soul," representing the oscillating sentiments of his compatriots. As a writer, political thinker, and emblem of uprooted Russian spirituality, he is a symbol of his nation's volatile, ambivalent relationship to the Jewish Question.

II A Concise Biography of Aleksandr Solzhenitsyn

To readers of this book, Solzhenitsyn's name and literary achievements will likely be familiar. However, a brief outline of the writer's biography will provide an historical backdrop to understand the pivotal events and publications of Aleksandr Isaeivich's creative life, as well as his role in contemporary Russo-Jewish history.

In 1918 Aleksandr Isaievich Solzhenitsyn was born in Koslovodsk, a resort town in the northern Caucusus. Thereafter, his middle-class family moved to the southern Russian port city of Rostov-on-Don, where he spent his adolescent years. The writer's father, an office worker, died before Aleksandr's birth; his mother, a schoolteacher, brought up the young boy. Solzhenitsyn's mother never remarried. She was an educated woman, fluent in French and English, and supported the small family as a typist and stenographer. They were obliged to rent rooms and huts from private owners because the state did not provide them with living space. After fifteen years, they were finally issued a modest room in a reconstructed stable.

From boyhood Solzhenitsyn desired to become a writer. As a young author, he submitted stories, all of which were rejected by the journal *Znamia*. Though he longed to study literature as his father had at Moscow University, his mother could not afford to send him to the capital. Thus he embarked upon a course of study in the Department of Physics and Mathematics at the University of Rostov-on-Don in 1937. Though mathematics was not his true love, it proved beneficial in future teaching capacities both in prison and following his sentence in exile. Ultimately, Solzhenitsyn was able to continue his literary studies concurrently with his mathematical education. To his great joy, by 1939 he was enrolled in a correspondence program of Moscow's Institute of History, Philosophy, and Literature. At this time, while still at the university, Solzhenitsyn married chemistry student Natalia Alekseevna Reshetovskaia.

In 1941 Nazi Germany invaded the Soviet Union. Hitler's three-million strong assault on the Eastern Front would ultimately drain the greater part of his resources. As a result of this colossal offensive, Solzhenitsyn found himself called to duty in the Red Army. Here, for the first time, his mathematical education truly shaped his destiny; he was transferred to artillery school and completed an abridged artillery training program in November of 1942. After his commissioning, he served for two weeks in the Gorky region before being made commander of a reconnaissance artillery battery on the Leningrad front. Serving continuously until 1945 in the battle of Kirks, in White Russia, in Poland, and in East Prussia, Solzhenitsyn was promoted to Captain and received the Order of the Patriotic War Class II and the Order of the Red Star.

During these years Solzhenitsyn corresponded with school friend N. D. Vitkevich, and criticized Stalin in his letters, albeit referring to the dictator under a pseudonym—"the man with the mustache." Unfortunately, Captain Solzhenitsyn's letters were intercepted and he was summoned to the office of brigade commander Colonel Travkin, where he was arrested. Drafts of stories were used to support a charge of anti-Soviet propaganda against Solzhenitsyn. He was beaten and interrogated at the infamous Lubianka Prison in Moscow, as well as sentenced in absentia (a common practice for the Soviet government) in 1945.

In all, Solzhenitsyn spent eight years in labor camps and internal exile. In the first five months he was confined to correctional camps near Moscow. Later in 1946, because of his mathematical expertise, the writer was relocated to a scientific research institute also in the capital where he would spend four years. During the three years remaining in his sentence Solzhenitsyn was sent to Ekibastuz, a new camp for political prisoners in Kazakhstan. He would later transform his experiences at that camp, working as a bricklayer, laborer, and smelter, into *Odin den' Ivan Denisovicha* (*One Day in the Life of Ivan Denisovich*). While imprisoned, he underwent surgery for a malignant tumor but was not told the diagnosis. He subsequently developed a recurrence, received radiotherapy in Tashkent, and recovered. This experience provided the setting for *Rakovy Korpus (Cancer Ward).* The hero, not unlike Solzhenitsyn himself, was a recently freed inmate of the Gulag. Solzhenitsyn tasted freedom from the labor camp nexus in early 1953, just prior to Stalin's death, and was exiled to rural Kazakhstan.

Rehabilitated in 1956 as a result of Khrushchev's reforms, he was allowed to settle in Riazan, a city in central Russia, where he found employment as a mathematics teacher. Here he commenced writing with renewed purpose and vigor.

Encouraged by the softening of ossified government restraints on cultural life—a hallmark of the de-Stalinization climate of the early 1960s—Solzhenitsyn submitted his short novel *One Day in the Life of Ivan Denisovich* to the leading Soviet literary periodical *Novy Mir* (*New World*) in 1962. The work has marginal relation to the Russo-Jewish Question but nevertheless provided the impetus which launched Solzhenitsyn's literary career. The novel quickly appeared in *Novy Mir*'s pages and was received with instant acclaim, rendering Solzhenitsyn an immediate literary icon. *Ivan Denisovich*, based on Solzhenitsyn's own forced-labor experiences, describes a typical day in the life of an inmate of a Stalinist forced-labor camp. Within a short period the novel produced a political sensation both abroad and in the Soviet Union. The book made an impression on the public with its simple yet *puissant* language and by the obvious authority with which it treated the daily privations and material hardships of camp life. All this was magnified by its seminal role as one of the first Soviet literary works of the post-Stalin era to realistically describe such life.

The period of state endorsement proved, however, to be ephemeral. Ideological constraints on cultural activity in the USSR hardened with Nikita Khrushchev's ouster in 1964, and Solzhenitsyn consequently met with increasing criticism and later with overt persecution by the authorities when he emerged as an "eloquent opponent" of authoritarian government policies. Following the publication of various short stories in 1963, Solzhenitsyn was denied further sanctioned publication of his work. He thus resorted to circulating them in the form of *samizdat* ("self-published") literature—i.e., as illegal literature circulated surreptitiously—as well as publication abroad.

The following years witnessed the foreign publication of a number of politically ambitious novels, reinforcing Solzhenitsyn's growing international reputation—especially in those nations where the Soviet one-party state was perceived as a menace. Further, the works provide provocative insights into the Russo-Jewish Question, the aspects of which will be discussed in a later chapter. *V kruge pervom* (*The First Circle*), written in 1968, was indirectly based on his years spent working in a prison research institute as a mathematician. The book portrays the sundry responses and ethical dilemmas of scientists at work on research for the secret police.

In 1970 Solzhenitsyn was awarded the Nobel Prize for Literature "for the ethical force with which he has pursued the indispensable traditions of Russian literature."[2] Carrying on the realistic tradition of the nineteenth century forged by literary figures such as Dostoevsky and Tolstoi, he has grown to be one of the twentieth century's most important writers. Yet even prior to receiving the prestigious award Solzhenitsyn was soon to publish a literary work that would shake the very foundations of the USSR.

Considered by many to be his magnum opus, *The Gulag Archipelago* caused a great stir both in the West and the USSR as a powerful indictment of Soviet crimes against humanity. The treatise was first published in Paris in the original Russian as *Arkhipelag GULag* in three volumes between 1973 and 1975. GULag—*Glavnoe Upravlenie Lagerei* (Chief Administration of the Labor Camps)—is a Russian acronym for the Soviet government agency that supervised the vast network of forced-labor camps. Solzhenitsyn used the word archipelago as a metaphor for the camps, which were scattered through the sea of civil society like a chain of islands extending from the Bering Strait almost to the Bosporus.

The work represented the author's attempt to compile a literary and historical record of the Soviet regime's thorough but deeply erratic use of terror against its own population. A testimonial to Stalinist atrocities, *The Gulag Archipelago* shocked readers outside the USSR with its chilling descriptions of Soviet brutality. The book gave new impetus to critics of the Soviet system and caused many sympathizers to question their position. *Gulag* remains a classic of world literature, the political implications of which are immeasurable. It also provides insight into Judeo-Russian dealings, adding pieces to this puzzle of history.

On 13 February 1974, Solzhenitsyn was deported from the USSR to West Germany and stripped of his Soviet citizenship. The KGB had discovered a manuscript for the first volume of *The Gulag Archipelago*. The recently-awarded Nobel Laureate first settled in Zürich, Switzerland, and later in Vermont, USA. While in the West, Solzhenitsyn completed *The Gulag Archi-*

---

2 http://www.nobelpreis.org/english/Literatur/solzhenitsyn.htm.

pelago; *Bodalsia telenok s dybom* (*The Oak and the Calf*), the memoirs of his last ten years in the Soviet Union; *The Mortal Danger: Misconceptions about Soviet Russia and the Threat to America*; and *Three Plays*. In 1989 an expanded version of *Avgust 1914* (*August 1914*) was published as the first in a projected series of novels about the Russian Revolution to be called, collectively, *Krasnoe Koleso* (*The Red Wheel*). Excerpts from this work were published in 1975 as *Lenin v Tsurike* (*Lenin in Zurich*). The years of toil invested in creating *The Red Wheel* further catalyzed latent desire to address the Jewish role in Russian history.

Following the dissolution of the Soviet Union, Solzhenitsyn left Vermont in 1994 and returned to his homeland. The new regime, led by Mikhail S. Gorbachëv, had offered to restore his citizenship already in 1990, and the next year his treason charges were formally expunged. With his triumphant homecoming Solzhenitsyn embarked on a heavily publicized tour through Siberia, becoming again a popular figure, though in favor with the extant authority this time around. He was later received by President Eltsin in 1994 and addressed the Russian *Duma* in that same year.

Since that time he has absconded from the public eye to complete his research of the Russo-Jewish Question with the publication of *Two Hundred Years Together*. In 2001 the writer published the first volume of the work, followed by the second in 2003. The desire to enter the perilous forest of Judeo-Russian relations in no less than a two-volume historical work has raised many eyebrows in literary and socio-historical circles. The writer is approaching ninety years in age and, consequently, this work will be among his last literary offerings to the world. Surely Solzhenitsyn is aware of this fact and hopes readers will share in his entreaty for Judeo-Russian healing.

Though revered and vilified for half a century, Solzhenitsyn's work has been among the most influential in modern literature.

III Judeophobia and the Jewish Question

The Jewish Question—the enigma of Jewish place in world history—finds itself at the core of political, philosophical, and artistic questions. What is more, as Tamas Ungvari has written, it is an historical concept used to describe circumstances of Jews in Western polities evolving as each respective nation's image and perception of the "Jew" evolves.[3] Creating an historical context for the Russo-Jewish Question is essential to appreciate its complexity. To do so one must initially turn to Jewish history within the greater European historical backdrop.

Historically the notion of a "Jewish Question" came into being as religious anti-Semitism gave way to secular (or what was termed intellectual) anti-Semitism of the Enlightenment era. The Enlightenment describes the period in European history (seventeenth–eighteenth century) when the ascendant philosophy declared that human reason, by means of rational thought, could alone answer difficult questions and serve as an ethical method for living. It had as its roots the scientific revolution of the late seventeenth century when scientists and philosophers such as Newton, Kepler, Galileo, Bacon, and Descartes advanced theories about the physical universe. Their discoveries directly contradicted and challenged the rule of the Catholic Church. In attacking both the superstition and non-secular rule of Western Europe, many scientists and philosophers of the Enlightenment also attacked Jews for their religious beliefs and separatist ways, pointing to them as a scapegoat for domestic problems.

Notwithstanding, this era of European history was one of relative tolerance toward Judaism. Napoleon Bonaparte looked favorably upon the Jews and liberated them from ghettos as he ravaged through Europe. Indeed, France's new Emperor sought to assimilate Jews into society with full equality, albeit stripping them of their religious identity in the process. Although Napoleon ultimately lost his wars and found himself in exile, the ideas he set in

---

3 Tamas Ungvari, *The Jewish Question in Europe*, (New York: Columbia University Press, 2000), 9.

motion had a tremendous ripple effect which reverberated in Russia as well. By the end of the nineteenth century the notion of keeping Jews as non-citizens was no longer defensible in the more liberal, socially tolerant environment of Europe.

The Age of Enlightenment also heralded the beginning of a new era in Russia's sociological history. The development of national cultures and enriched relations with Western Europe brought much change to Russian society, education, science, literature, and art. In this regard Russia entered into a full cultural exchange with the rest of its European neighbors. The monarchy played a major role in this transition toward more modern times in Russia, actively participating in the evolution taking place in Russian social, cultural, and political life. One of the most important changes caused by this increased interaction and exchange within Europe was the shift from feudal orders to a capitalist system. This change paved the way for further social developments in Russia, which in turn stimulated the intellectual elite. There were few intellectuals, artists, scientists, or writers who did not contribute to solving the social problems of the day, the Jewish Question being an issue of great import.

To place Russia's Jewish Question in historical context one must understand the pivotal events of Russian history that have contributed to Judeophobia and modern anti-Semitism. The earlier Tsarist history of Russian Jewry is given in-depth analysis in the first tome of Solzhenitsyn's *Two Hundred Years Together* but is beyond the scope of this thesis. Nonetheless, fundamental knowledge of this history is essential to understanding the nuances of the Post-Soviet Russo-Jewish Question. Historian Stanley Mann renders a detailed picture of Jewish existence in Tsarist Russia; whilst assuming a melancholy tone there is also a note of nostalgia on the part of Jews toward the country of their birth.

> Its cities are called the Paris of the Baltic. It's a vast country—a country of harsh winters that stopped foreign invaders and wild winds that bring in the autumn rain, fine and chill. It's banishments to the desolates and souls that languished. It's forced silence and stirring music. It's long train rides into the vast Steppes. It's a country where in winter hot tea is sold in the streets—and lemonade in the summer. It's War and Peace, and short stories. It's a land where an Empress banished her personal

> physician of eighteen years upon learning that he was a Jew and a leader of today who comes to the ceremony to light the Chanukah Menorah candles. It's a land of exodus and pogroms. It's sweet and sad balalaika music. It's partisans and love for the motherland. It's Yiddish not suppressed but still spoken and knocks on the door. It's Tchaikovsky and Rimsky-Korsakov. It's Tsarist decrees that forced its Jewish citizens to serve its armies for forty years. It's old buildings gilded and brief rays of sunshine. It's skies huge and domed and a curtain that once was iron. It's Russia.[4]

Although it is clearly a sentimental piece, Mann suggests the Jewish ambivalence towards Russia through polarized expressions.

Let us examine the expression: Russia's Jewish Question. Jewish historian Iosef Bikermann writes: "Но жить среди чужих народов ещё значит и жить в чужих *государствах — В этом сущность еврейского вопроса.*"[5] Judaism initially had an influence on Russian culture and social climate in the sixteenth century, not long after the expulsion of the Jews from Spain by Queen Isabella in 1492. In subsequent centuries, scores of Jews migrated to Poland, Lithuania, Ukraine, and Belorussia. Anti-Semitism trailed after the Jews from Western Europe and by the sixteenth century Muscovy already espoused a strong element of that prejudice.

During the century following the Polish partition, Jews were to increase fivefold. Their work ethic, sense of community, and education made them real competitors, well suited to reap the benefits of Russia's economic development during the nineteenth century. Historian Geoffrey Hosking explains that many Jews engaged in pursuits such as tax and liquor-farming, sugar-refining, and the grain and timber trade. Further, Jews were in leading positions in the railways, banking, newspapers, and professions of culture. The so-called Pale of Settlement in the west and south, to which most of them were confined, proved extremely porous in practice, and not only because of exemptions for the wealthy and educated; the salaries of some big-city police

---

4 Stanley Mann, „It Had its History," http://www.wzo.org.il/en/resources/view.asp?id=1547&subject=131 (as of 20 April 2005).

5 Iosef. M. Bikerman, *K samopoznaniu evreia: Chem my byli, chem my stali, chem, my dolzhny byt'*, (Paris: n.p., 1939), 64.

officers were probably exceeded by the backhanders they received from Jews living illegally.[6]

During the nineteenth century, restrictions on the Jewish population were alternately eased and tightened. Tsar Alexander II, for example, relaxed restrictions on settlement, education, and employment. His assassination in 1881, however, brought reimposition of all previous restrictions, which then remained in force until the fall of the monarchy in 1917. During that period Jews were abused, killed, and plundered in pogroms led by a group called the Black Hundred (a movement which will be given greater attention in a subsequent section). Despite exploitive circumstances in Russia and high levels of emigration to America, the Jewish population burgeoned in the nineteenth century; by the outbreak of the First World War, an estimated 5.2 million Jews lived in Russia.

Jews played a considerable role in the economic and political development of the Russian Empire, not to mention notable representation in the revolutionary movement which rose up to challenge the Russian Monarchical dynasty. Anti-Semitism—or Judeophobia, which was the more common expression in Tsarist Russia—became an important element of Russian conservative thought. Ultimately the Russo-Jewish Question is an inquiry into the place and role of Jews in contemporary Russian society, based on an analysis of the symbiotic relationship of both races throughout history.

On the threshold of the October Revolution, the Russian Empire housed the largest population of Jews in the world. For many years Jews were restricted to the Pale of Settlement in the westernmost reaches of the Russian Empire. At this time, many facets of modern intellectual Judaic thought, including Zionism, Territorialism, and Jewish forms of socialism, had their genesis in Russia and other regions of Eastern Europe. Thus Russian Jews were not unlike their Diaspora kinsmen who progressed to be a salient caste in whichever nation their lot was cast. The Jewish Question eventually became one of the most divisive politico-social issues in the Russian Empire during the course of the entire nineteenth century. Indeed, it seemed to be the hinge upon which Russian history turned. Using this metaphor the pre-

---

6 Geoffrey Hosking, „Aleksandr Solzhenitsyn, Dvesti let vmeste, Russki Put," *Johnson's Russia List*, 5 March 2002.

eminent Russian philosopher Nikolai Berdiaev wrote concerning the Jewish role in world history and religion:

> Еврейский вопрос... это ось, вокруг которой вращается религиозная история. Таинственна историческая судьба евреев... Ни один народ в мире не пережил бы столь долгого рассеяния и наверное потерял бы своё лицо и растворился бы среди других народов. Но по неисповедимым путям Божьим народ этот должен сохраниться до конца времён. Менее всего, конечно, можно было бы объяснить историческую судьбу еврейства с точки зрения атериалистического понимания истории.[7]

One of the consequences of the October Revolution and subsequent Civil War was the eruption of virulent anti-Semitism in Russia. Just as socialism was the ideology of the intelligentsia, and nationalism was that of the old civil and military establishment, so Judeophobia might be said to have become the ideology of the Russian masses. At the conclusion of the Civil War, hatred of Jews was one of the foremost features of contemporary Russian life—possibly even the most prominent because a large stratum ignorantly saw Jews as the sole arbiter of Communism which, incidentally, had brought civil war to their homeland.

The widely nurtured anti-Semitism of national-religious chauvinism which developed in twentieth-century Europe (Russia included) was, in fact, centuries old. The term *anti-Semitism*, however, is perhaps inappropriate; despite its prefix, the term reflects an idea without any clear opposite, implying that *Semitism* exists in opposition to it. This, of course, is not the case. The term no doubt produces a political undertone although it has little to no logical underpinning. *Anti-Judaism*, similar to Judeophobia, would arguably be a more precise term in that such discrimination has historical origin in the religious-cultural antipathy between Christianity and Judaism. In the twentieth century, however, such antipathy has grown into a complex beast fed by modern totalitarian ideologies. Despite these semantic problems, the common term "anti-Semitism" will be used throughout this work to denote antipa-

---

7 Nikolai Berdiaev, *Khristianstvo i antisemitizm: (Religioznaia sud'ba evreistva)* (Paris: Izdanie Religiozno-Filisofskoi akademii,1938), 4–5.

thy towards and persecution of Jews in Russia and the allegations raised by Solzhenitsyn's work.

IV Anti-Semitic Accusation against Solzhenitsyn

Solzhenitsyn's personal history of anti-Semitic accusation reaches surprisingly early into his youth. Experiences during the writer's formative years rise to the surface at times in his literature, especially those relating to the young man's relations with Jewish schoolmates. More importantly, such memories may be subconsciously indicative of his feelings regarding the Jewish role in Russian history. To illustrate, let us consider several examples from Solzhenitsyn's formative years. Early on, the future writer had traumatic experiences when he began encountering religious persecution:

> At the age of ten he had had the cross ripped from his neck by jeering Pioneers, and for over a year he was held up to ridicule at school meetings and told that he ought to join. He was used to regarding himself as 'different' from the other children and to standing somewhat apart, but eventually the need to conform proved greater than his urge for a difficult independence. But it was not a simple matter, for the crosscurrents in the school were rather complex. It would appear that the principal activists in the Pioneer and Komsomol movements, at least in Rostov, were Jewish children, whose parents had been systematically discriminated against under the Tsarist regime. They were naturally enthusiastic about the new order, but the fact of their nationality endowed Solzhenitsyn's cross with a certain ambiguity.[8]

It should not be forgotten that Solzhenitsyn himself would subsequently identify with Marxism-Leninism for a time, but the above event undoubtedly struck a chord which resonated beyond his youth. Also as an adolescent he was not unaware of common slur against Jewish lads engaged in school ground scuffles. On one such occasion Aleksandr remarked that "everybody has the right to speak his mind" when asked which of two fighting boys (one of whom was Jewish) he supported after the Jewish lad had been racially in-

8 Aleksandr Solzhenitsyn, *Skvoz' Chad* (Paris: YMCA Press, 1979), 64.

sulted. Hereafter the young writer was labeled an anti-Semite amongst his classmates.[9] Such an occurrence apparently etched itself deep enough into his memory to later find a fictional place in his book *The First Circle*. Yet even further back down Solzhenitsyn's memory lane we find him brawling with one Alexander Kagan over a sheath knife. Solzhenitsyn bumped his head and received a scar, which remained on his forehead thereafter. This incident seems harmless enough but it would later be the subject of defamatory attempts to discredit the writer morally and was even used in claims of anti-Semitism by Soviet authorities (to be further discussed subsequently) following his expulsion from the homeland.

As young Solzhenitsyn came of age his perceptions of Russian Jewry changed for a time as he became evermore conditioned by the evolving political climate surrounding him. By his early adolescence he was having progressively less to do with the family circle of his childhood. Bolshevism was in theory impartial to nationality and consequently Jews, finding many Tsarist era glass ceilings were lifted, assumed a new place in Communist Russia. Although gradually relinquishing the Orthodoxy and culture of his upbringing, Solzhenitsyn was influenced by the new political movements and ultimately embraced a Marxist, atheistic worldview. In an interview he states: "The party had become our father, and we—the children—obeyed. So, when I was leaving school and embarking on my time at university, I made a choice: I banished all my childhood misgivings. I was a Communist. The world would be what we made of it."[10] Historically this whirlwind of new political ideology had great influence on the rising generation and thus it is difficult to grasp the psychological process of young Aleksandr in espousing Bolshevism. Biographer Michael Scammell suggests Solzhenitsyn's conversion was slow, but convert he did. This reluctance may have been attributed in part to early disenchantment with the Soviet regime, such as the body-search to which his grandfather was subjected by the OGPU and the incarceration of his father-figure, Vladimir Fedorovsky. The writer commented, "Man is the most complex creature on earth . . . I am incapable of describing the role of my uncon-

9 Michael Scammell, *Solzhenitsyn: A Biography* (London: Paladin Grafton Books, 1984), 65.

10 „Solzhenitsyn in Zurich—an interview," *Encounter* 271 (1976), 11.

scious during the '30s or thereabouts."[11] Although Solzhenitsyn as a political prisoner gradually came to vehemently reject all things Marxist-Leninist and their ideological cascade across Russia, for a time he did identify with Marx (who was, of course, Jewish) and temporarily became united with the Bolshevism of his school-day Judeo-atheist classmates.

There is reason to believe that at this time in Solzhenitsyn's life his mind became imbued with certain associations between Judaism and Communism. However, what this means for him as far as self-identity is highly speculative. Some, including Russian nationalist Ivan Samolvin and scholar Daniel Rancour-Laferrière, go so far as to suggest that a type of "shadow identity" or "crypto-Jewishness" began taking form during these years reflected both in his writing and in the attacks that would later be leveled at him by the Soviet authorities.

With Solzhenitsyn's international acclaim in the 1960s, both as a writer and as a political opponent of the Soviet Union, came sundry attempts to vilify his name from various politico-cultural angles. The censure which ensued assumed a most unexpected tone with efforts to label the writer either a virulent anti-Semite—advocating the timeless blood libel of Judeo-Masonic conspiracy—or a philo-Semitic Jewish Zionist, depending on the political demands of the party. The theory that Solzhenitsyn possesses a latent, crypto-Jewish nature seems bewildering but was included in the controversy by Soviet officials who mounted criticism against him. On the domestic front, party officials colluded to trump up the writer's alleged surreptitious Judaic identity among the Russian nationalist demographic. The story of how his father Isaaky Lazhenitsyn's racial identity was questioned by Kharkov University prompted the KGB to attempt to prove Solzhenitsyn was in reality Jewish:

> A special major of the state security named Blagovidov rushed off to check the personal files of all the Isaakys on the archives of Moscow University for tempting possible 'explanation' of my literary position. After all, with the appearance of my historical novel (*August 1914*), the task of my pursuers grows complicated: it is not enough to defame the author; it is necessary also to undermine trust in his views of Russian

---

11 Ibid.

> history—those he has already expressed and those he may express in the future. Alas, the racist researchers were thwarted: I turned out to be a Russian.[12]

Strangely enough many mutations of Aleksandr Isaevich's surname have been concocted to defame the writer, though such rumors were not necessarily spread with an anti-Semitic intent. For example when David Markish was visiting Argentina in the 1970s he encountered an elderly Jew who queried Markish in the following way:

> 'How's that, you know, what's his name . . . Solzhenichkin, Smolzhenichkin . . . that writer? How's he getting on over there? Does he go to the synagogue every day?' I was somewhat taken aback.
> 'Solzhenitsyn is a Russian,' I said, 'and a devout Christian. He's living in Switzerland.'
> 'Don't give me that!' replied the old man with a sly wink. 'No use defending him! I know for sure!'[13]

Indeed the confidence of the elderly Jewish gentleman in his own knowledge of Solzhenitsyn's "true" identity is the stuff from which anti-Semitism is made. Further untruths began to spread that his surname was really "Solzhenitser," the son of a Jewish father. This misnomer occurred at an ideological lecture presented in a Moscow publishing house where a speaker disparaged the writer by referring to him continually as "Solzhenitser." When the speaker was informed that he was pronouncing the writer's surname incorrectly, he replied, "No it's not a mistake. The person known to you as Solzhenitsyn is really Solzhenitser and he's a Jew."[14] What is more, it did not help that the author's patronymic, Isaevich (adopted instead of the usual Isaakievich), sounds like the Old Testament Jewish prophet Isaiah. Exacerbating the situation further, certain Jews themselves believed that Solzhenitsyn was in fact Jewish.

---

12 Aleksandr Solzhenitsyn, *The Oak and the Calf: Sketches of Literary Life in the Soviet Union*, trans. Harry Willetts (New York: Harper & Row, 1979), 508.

13 David Markish, „V strane moloka i miasa," *Sion* 12 (1975) 116–117.

14 Zhores Medvedev, *Ten Years After Ivan Denisovich*, trans. Hilary Sternberg (New York: Vintage Books, 1974), 100.

The drama of the Soviet state's attempts to label Solzhenitsyn an anti-Semite stemmed from the same political agenda mentioned previously, but used the other side of the Jewish coin. The earliest charges of this sort appearing in articles of the *Jerusalem Post* in the early 1970s included Soviet émigré Mikhail Grobman (of Jewish decent) whose writing acted as a catalyst for subsequent articles of a similar tenor. Following this trend of accusation and especially after the writer's receiving of the Nobel Prize in 1974, the Soviet media and intelligence community devised new methods of persecution, labeling Solzhenitsyn a "monarcho-fascist-chauvinist" and painting him an anti-Semite. The first examples of this appeared in Western media, which was influenced by the Israeli, Russian émigré, and American presses. Despite vehement denials of any tinge of anti-Semitism, Solzhenitsyn's seemingly audacious public statements and literary treatment of Jewish historical characters often came back to haunt him. He expounds on the term "anti-Semitism":

> This word, just as other labels as well, has lost its precise meaning from thoughtless use, and different publicists in different decades understood it differently. If a biased and unjustified attitude toward the Jewish nation is understood by this term—then I tell you assuredly: not only is there no—nor could there be—'anti-Semitism' in my work, nor for that matter in any book worthy of being called literature. To approach a literary work with the measuring stick of anti-Semitism is vulgar, an underdeveloped understanding of the nature of a literary work. By this measuring stick Shakespeare could be proclaimed anti-Semitic, and his creative work struck out.[15]

What is curious but by no means aberrant in terms of modern media practices is the manner in which the wrangling bids farewell to all sense of reason and trespasses into the ridiculous and illogical. Dr. Michael Nicholson explains: "In the controversy over Solzhenitsyn's alleged anti-Semitism the occasional instances of vitriol and bluster are less curious than those mo-

15 Aleksandr Solzhenitsyn, quoted in Richard Grenier, „Solzhenitsyn and Anti-Semitism: A New Debate; Expanded Novel Prompts Dispute," *New York Times*, 13 November 1985, C21.

ments when polemic slips the bonds of reality altogether. Since the Soviet information agencies owe allegiance to no principle higher than expediency, it is inappropriate to expect them to be inhibited by any sense of the absurd: for them Solzhenitsyn will be an anti-Russian Jew or anti-Jewish Russian, or both, as the occasion demands."[16]

One of the most fanatical of all Solzhenitsyn's enemies was Grigorii Klimov. The latter published a work in 1974 entitled *Case No. 69. On Psychological Warfare, Mad-Houses, the third Jewmigration and the Forces of Darkness.* Klimov's personal convictions included Jewish conspiracy theories wrapped up in Ziono-Masonic collusions. In Klimov's eyes, Solzhenitsyn embodies Judaism at some level, being married to a half-Jewess, then to a full Jewess; in the guise of a Russian and an Orthodox Christian Solzhenitsyn "proclaims the total dismemberment of Mother Russia and, like the Antichrist, crows over her ruin, echoing the dreams of all Russia's foes."[17]

Whilst the Soviet regime's reckless attempts to sully the exiled writer leave little to the imagination, Solzhenitsyn has at times aggravated his own image by committing literary *faux pas* in an already sensitive Jewish area. Although receiving acclaim internationally, his intentions were questioned when in 1977 volume II of *The Gulag Archipelago* appeared with six photographs of some of the camps' most sadistic administrators. However, among the scores of complicit Gulag murderers (Russians included) the author had chosen only the faces of Jews (in a country where Jews make up about 4% of the population). Due to the general paucity of images in the work, these photos stuck out immensely. These individuals included: Aron Solts, Jakov Rappaport, Matvei Berman, Lazar Kogan and, most notorious of all, Naftaly Frenkel, who is purported to have master-minded the whole technique of slave labor. Even if they had been the only pictures available, many criticize the author's judgment in including them. Scammell writes concerning the images:

> Skeptical readers pointed out that there were many more purely Russian administrators in the Gulag than Jewish ones, that they were not a

---

16 Michael Nicholson, „Effigies and Oddities," *Solzhenitsyn in Exile*, ed. J. Dunlop et al. (Stanford: Hoover Institution Press, 1985), 123.

17 Grigorii Klimov, *Case No. 69. On Psychological Warfare, Mad-Houses, the Third Jewmigration and the Forces of Darkness* (Woodridge, NY: Slavia,1974), 105.

> wit less cruel or sadistic than their Jewish colleagues, and that it could hardly be a coincidence that Solzhenitsyn laid so much emphasis on Jews, not to mention in his photographs, but also in his text. The question was, Did Solzhenitsyn do it deliberately, had it come about unconsciously, or had he been 'fed' this information and fallen into a trap?[18]

Are anti-Semitic accusations against Solzhenitsyn just? Yes and no. While there is much to indicate his respect and even affection for Jews, the writer has written and uttered words that may be interpreted as anti-Jewish at some level. What makes Solzhenitsyn intriguing is that there is ambivalence in *his* Jewish Question, which is evident in thorough surveys of his writing—likely the best source to divine his inner, subconscious beliefs about Jews because an artistic work so often exhibits the most objective glimpse into the soul.

---

18 Scammell, *Solzhenitsyn*, 959.

V Russian Nationalism

As the 1970s came to a close the discussion of Solzhenitsyn's alleged anti-Semitism was overshadowed by a broader debate regarding the writer's nationalism. One of the arguments imputing anti-Jewish views to Solzhenitsyn is that his fervent love of Russia un-masks his "real" anti-Semitic person. As was made apparent in various writings and especially in his *Letter to Soviet Leaders*, the writer longs for the spiritual (even metaphysical) Orthodox Russia of times past. What can be easily misconstrued is that this past era was also one of pogroms and Jewish persecution. In history it may appear that there is a link between Russian Orthodoxy and Russian nationalism that reserves anti-Semitism as its logical outlet of discrimination.

Whilst passionate observers of Russian Orthodoxy relate to Jews as to any other religious minority, extreme Russian nationalists devote a great deal of thought to Jews, namely in what ways the latter have apparently caused harm to Russia. For the overly-zealous Orthodox nationalist, Jews are not just an object for racial antipathy among other ethnic minorities in the "alien" class, such as Georgians, Chechens, Poles, Germans, Armenians, Uzbeks, or Americans. Rather the Jews or Judaism constitutes the source from which Christianity, namely Orthodox Christianity, was born and which the former rejected. Hence there exists the potential for special antipathy towards Jews among Russians who are nationalist enough to be aware of their Orthodox roots but not Christian enough to realize that such racism does not fall into traditional New Testament interpretations of "love thy neighbour." Where Solzhenitsyn falls among these groups has been widely debated. Daniel Rancour-Laferrière writes about the particular place of anti-Jewish tradition found in Russia:

> Russians have thus always been somewhat more prepared to hate Jews than to hate other nationalities. This is not to deny that they have hated other nationalities with great intensity too in certain situations, e.g., Chechens during the recent conflicts in Chechnia. But anti-

> Chechen prejudice is something different. While the cliché 'traditional Russian anti-Semitism' is to some extent justified, an expression such as 'traditional Russian anti-Chechenism' would sound bizarre and would not be justified on either historical or psychological grounds. Similarly, there is a strong tendency for nationalists to link the 'Russian Question' to the 'Jewish Question,' but one would never find the 'Russian Question' linked to the 'Chechen Question.'[19]

The growing disenchantment with capitalism in present-day Russia has further sowed hostility towards the West, spawning new hues of nationalism. These contemporary strains of nationalism have a different interpretation for the perceived antipathy between Russia and the West. Many of today's Russian extreme nationalists assert that everything the West has exported to their country is detrimental because (in their view) Russia and the West come from two disparate civilizations. Unfortunately Solzhenitsyn's patriotic disposition has been interpreted in the West as ultra-right by some and fascist by others. Consequently, his name comes up when politically extreme movements begin agitating anti-Semitic opinion in Russia and even in the West.

Though it is ironic considering Russia's historic struggle with Nazi Germany, post-Soviet Russia has indeed witnessed an increase in Fascist ideology with sympathies for Hitler and the swastika. Evgeny Proshechkin, the chairman of Moscow's Anti-Fascist Center, writes:

> The process of infiltrating fascism into the public conscience and the public itself is now under way in Russia. This process is proceeding in geometrical progression. A few years ago, a person would have felt very uncomfortable if somebody had said to him, 'In fact, your views are close to fascism, this is fascism.' But now, millions of Russians are ready to respond, 'What is wrong with fascism? It is just respect for the national feelings.' I think a dangerous event has occurred—a sharp turn in the public conscience to the belief that fascism is something good.[20]

---

19 Daniel Rancour-Laferrière, „Imagining Russia: Ethnic Identity and the Nationalist Mind," http://www.panorama.ru/works/patr/ir/ (as of 7 November 2003).

20 Semyon Reznick, *The Nazification of Russia* (Washington D.C.: Challenge Publications, 1996), 248.

Many neo-Fascist groups have surfaced in the wake of economic instability attacking all ethnic minority groups, especially Jews. However, such burgeoning anti-Jewish prejudice on the part of neo-Fascist Russians diverges from that of its Soviet predecessors. Their aims are not simply to limit Jewish influence in Russia, but to deport or exterminate Jews altogether. This overtly fanatical persecution, it has been suggested, was never as widespread, even in the Tsarist era. For instance, Dmitri Shlapentokh states in "The World and I" that there is little to no difference between the views of the educated and the uneducated or the young and the old regarding anti-Semitic feelings.[21]

It is arguable that nationalism—due to its extremist proclivities—has proven deleterious to Russia as she struggles to redefine herself following seven decades of communist rule. The history of the Russian far right traces back to nineteenth-century religious groups and theorists, such as St. John of Kronstadt who defended the Tsar against political and ideological groups deemed nefarious to Imperial Russia. Central to the mentality of the Russian far right was (and in some cases still is) that Jews, Freemasons, socialist liberals, and American or Western European capitalists pose a threat to "Holy Mother Russia."

It is worth devoting a few words to extremist Russian nationalism so as to understand Solzhenitsyn's clear distance from it. To be sure, the vast topic of Russia's radical right demands its own research, but this work will merely touch upon it with regard to Solzhenitsyn and anti-Semitism.

The Black Hundred

Numerous reactionary, anti-revolutionary, anti-Semitic groups formed in Russia during and after the Russian Revolution of 1905. Among such was the Black Hundred (*Chernosotentsy),* a conservative-nationalist party. Favoring Tsarism and Autocracy rather than parliamentary government, the Black Hundred were the perpetrators of many Jewish pogroms in Russian cities

21 Dmitri Shlapentokh, „The Fate of the Jews in Post-Soviet Russia," *The World and I*, 19:4 (2000), 284.

such as Odessa, Kiev, Ekaterinoslav, and Bialystok. This group of radicals increased in popularity before the beginning of the Russian Revolution as Tsarism began to diminish. The Black Hundred believed that "all Jews were revolutionaries and all revolutionaries were Jews, all Jews were capitalists and all capitalists were either Jews or tools in the hands of Jews."[22] In spite of the latter belief, only a small fraction of Jews were actually capitalists. What is more, Jews were a minority in most Russian cities. However, their absence did not alter the mindset of the Black Hundred; according to them, the Jew is an Anarchist, absent and yet ubiquitous, an emotive myth helping to marshal the ignorant masses.

What distinguished the traditional right with groups under the umbrella of the Black Hundred was the latter's great attention dedicated to the Jewish Question. It is important to understand that those on the moderate or traditional right were neither gracious to Jews nor warm to the notion of establishing equal rights for them. However, as Laqueur expounds: "For the traditional right-wing parties, all of which had been anti-Semitic to some extent, the 'Jewish problem' had been just one of a number of issues, domestic and foreign, such as Slavophilism, foreign political expansion (especially toward the south), the strengthening of the Russian armed forces, and so on."[23] In contrast, the Black Hundred expressed a form of ethnocentric Russian nationalism, having no sympathy for even fellow Slavs. In this fanatical vision all Western European nations, especially France and Britain, had been "Judaized." What is more, the Black Hundred were isolationists, calling for reductions of armed forces spending. Above all they reserved vehement prejudice for Jews who were deemed the "source of all evil in holy Russia." In the mind of a Black Hundred adherent, every Jew was a communist and vice versa. Of course, the centuries-long stereotype of the "Jewish capitalist" could not be erased. Indeed, the Black Hundred, as mentioned, fostered the contradictory belief that Jews were simultaneously capitalist and communist: Genadi Shimanov, a leading face of the extreme right since *perestroika*, has argued that capitalism, even before the Christian era, had been an invention of the Jews,

---

22 Walter Laqueur, *Black Hundred; The Rise of the Extreme Right in Russia* (New York: HarperCollins Publishers, 1993) 26.

23 Ibid., 26.

who also conceived Communism; their dominion over world finance has been and is the key to their domination of the world.[24]

But the Black Hundred should be understood for what they truly were—neither a political movement nor a party, but a nebulous, xenophobic psyche embodying sundry right-wing groups active around and after the turn of the twentieth century. Thus they symbolized not an ephemeral ideology but a certain element of Russian psyche. Semyon Frank writes: "'Black Hundredism' refers not just to a specific political group but to 'a matter of morals and character which had deeper roots: It is rooted in the primordial darkness of the Russian soul, its unenlightened deposits.'"[25] The dark corner of nationalistic pathos embodied in Black Hundredism provides a backdrop and a starting point to understanding the anti-Judaic extreme right-wing of Russia.

National Bolshevism

The National Bolshevism movement warrants consideration in the milieu of Russia's extremist ethnocentric tendencies. Historically it emerged almost simultaneously in Russia and Germany. Within the Russian context, National Bolshevism was a widespread name for Communists who sought to secure the integrity of state and (either consciously or subconsciously) continued the "Great Russian historical mission" of establishing geopolitical preeminence. In Germany the analogous phenomenon materialized in extremely left forms of nationalism during the 1920s and 30s, in which the ideas of non-orthodox socialism—the national idea and positive attitude to Soviet Russia—were fused. National Bolshevism had a rebirth of sorts in the 1960s and 70s and has developed further since the Soviet Union's collapse. John Dunlop outlines the National Bolsheviks' chief features as: a quasi-deification of the Russian people, suspicion of a Jewish-Masonic-Plutocratic conspiracy, and a feeling of extreme hostility towards the West. He further describes the movement: "The similarities between National Bolshevism are striking: a strong impulse toward deification of the nation; the desire for a strong state, the *stato totalitario*; a powerful leadership impulse; . . . a belief in the necessity of an elite; a cult of

24 Genadi Shimanov, „O tainoi prirode kapitalizma," *Veche* 10, (1991).
25 Laqueur, *Black Hundred*, xvi.

discipline, particularly of the youth; heroic vitalism; an acceptance of military might; . . . and a celebration of the glories of the past."[26]

National Bolshevism had a renaissance in the late 1960s in conjunction with the Chalmaiev affair. The latter was an obscure journalist of *Molodaia Gvardia* whose incendiary articles redefined the National Bolshevik movement. The premise of Chalmaiev's writing could be described as a reactionary muddle of confused Marxism and Russian nationalism—indeed an uncanny amalgam of ideologically contradictory ideas. As the Chalmaiev affair gained attention it divided Soviet intellectuals, although Solzhenitsyn did not voice support for National Bolsheviks or left-wing Marxists who opposed the movement. Michael Scammell describes National Bolshevism as:

> A reactionary mishmash of Brezhnev-style Communism and old-fashioned Russian chauvinism with Slavophile overtones—a mixture that was sometimes dubbed 'National Bolshevism' (by analogy with National Socialism) by its opponents, although it was then just beginning to be formulated. The West was denounced as hopelessly corrupt and degenerate, 'choking on a surfeit of hate' and the fount of all evil. . . . The Russian tradition, on the other hand, was pure and lofty, fed by a 'sacred spring.' It had degenerated somewhat under the trivializing impact of television, the cinema, the mass media (all imports from the West), but it could reform itself by turning back to its roots, drawing inspiration from the Russian village, the moral and spiritual values of the Russian people, the pure idioms of popular speech. There were mystic references to the sacramental power of the native soil, even an invocation of Holy Russia, her saints and just men born of a yearning for miracles and loving kindness.[27]

The contemporary ideology of National Bolshevism espouses a Utopian path to reach its ends: Great Europa/State Eurasia—the political union and merging of Europe and Russia into a Geopolitical and economical block—to oppose the United States and its alleged materialist cosmopolitanism. As present-day National Bolsheviks declare on their website: "The political aim of

---

26 John Dunlop, *The New Russian Nationalism* (New York: Praeger, 1985), 88–89.
27 Scammell, *Solzhenitsyn*, 669.

National Bolshevism is therefore revolution on the social, regional, political, and economical level in Eurasia on a global scale; the national revolutions in all countries in the spectrum from Gibraltar to Vladivostok."[28]

Because National Bolshevism claims to be the antithesis of capitalism and all the latter's Liberal-materialist values, its core values are Socialist and Traditionalist. From this point of origin, National Bolshevism uses the Hegelian triad (thesis + antithesis = synthesis) to formulate a clear, distinctive National-Bolshevik political philosophy. It is not Communist, Fascist, Democratic, or anything else; instead it takes these antithetic ideologies and combines them to form a new Socialist soup. National Bolshevism breaks the ideological isolationism by combining ideals of opposite ideologies, thoughts, and traditions, thus forming a synthesis philosophy.

Interestingly enough, certain Jews have shown support for National Bolshevism, such as critic I. Lezhnev. The latter proclaimed: "Russian imperialism (from ocean to ocean), Russian messianism (*ex oriente lux*), and Russian Bolshevism (on the world scale), are all magnitudes of the same dimension."[29] Lezhnev was among the stratum of Jews which fervently sought Russian identity, albeit without adopting Orthodoxy. He embraced Marxism in the 1930s and made a career for himself in the Soviet Press.

It is noteworthy that National Bolshevism does in fact espouse parallels with Solzhenitsyn's veneration of the Russian homeland—for example, the movement's praise of Orthodoxy and Russian Saints; the nostalgia for village culture and Russian national tradition; and the appeal to Russian, as opposed to Soviet, patriotism.

Where the writer categorically disagrees with this movement is in its interpretation of the October Revolution, which is seen by National Bolshevism as the culmination of Russian history. Solzhenitsyn emphatically contends that the events of 1917 transpired as a result of Western European influence, namely German political philosophy. In essence, Solzhenitsyn attacks what he deems a spiritual deficit of the movement which vehemently defends the purity and Russianness of the Petersburg and neo-Muscovite Soviet periods

---

28 Thomas Sutter, „What's National-Bolshevism? Philosophical Basis & Metaphysic Heritage [Summary]," http://www.bolsheviks.org/DOCUMENTS/WHAT.htm (as of 20 April 2005).

29 Quoted in M. Agurskii, *The Third Rome: National Bolshevism in the USSR* (Boulder: West View Press, 1987), xv.

of Russian history. But they mock the historically penitential Russian psyche, which Solzhenitsyn considers an inherent (if latent) element of Russian national consciousness. What is more, he feels that National Bolshevism is an ideological debasement of patriotism. This he outlined in the final section of "Repentance and Self-Limitation in the Life of Nations." To be sure, he condemned the movement's overwhelming condescension for all things Western, its xenophobic fulminations against Masons and Jews, and even its excessive veneration of Russia. Daniel Mahoney, in defense of Solzhenitsyn, writes:

> They [the National Bolsheviks] share a narrowly racist or ethnic view of what it means to be Russian in contrast to Solzhenitsyn's own capacious emphasis on the spiritual, cultural, and political preconditions of Russian national identity. . . . It is clear that Solzhenitsyn considers the temptation of National Bolshevism to be one of the fundamental obstacles to the recovery of a healthy national life rooted in repentance and self-limitation.[30]

Память

A more contemporary resurgence of Russian "new right" nationalism is the movement known as *Память* (Memory)—an ultra-nationalist and overtly anti-Semitic organization identifying itself as the "People's National-Patriotic Orthodox Christian movement." *Память* is not a cohesive political party nor is it another far-right organization, but a circa 1980s amalgam of several right wing groups with ideological parallels. To be sure, generalizing about *Память* is problematic not only by virtue of its many schisms, but also because it has sought to be a movement rather than a political party with a cogent ideology.

The *Память* assembly was apparently inspired by the novel *Память*, published in 1982 by Chivilikhin. Although the movement's doctrine has been difficult to pin down due to disparate voices among the leadership, the following constitutes the fundamental tenets of the organization's core beliefs.

---

30 Daniel Mahoney, *Aleksandr Solzhenitsyn: The Ascent from Ideology* (Lanham: Roman & Littlefield, 2001), 117.

Память denies the legality of Russia's incumbent power due to its succession from the "illegal" October Revolution of 1917; in spite of this it does capitulate to the present administration. *Память* regards the overthrow of monarchy as a realization of Ziono-Masonic collusion against Russia. Further, the movement regards Communism as a doctrine of the Talmud and democracy as a precursor to the advent of the Jewish emperor, as described in *The Protocols of the Elders of Zion*. *Память* appeals to all "genuine patriots" of the motherland to unite and restore the Autocratic Monarchy of Russia.[31]

The platform of *Память* has been delineated by John Dunlop. The latter sought out and interviewed the erstwhile leader of *Память*, Dmitrii Vasiliev, and claims the main tenets are three: absolute monarchy, re-establishment of the Russian Orthodox Church, and "nationality" (an ambiguous point regarding the titular nation's right to have a consular role in the Russian state's affairs). Beyond that, there is a preoccupation with traditional folk heroes such as Alexander Nevsky, Emilian Pugachëv, and Pyotr Stolypin. *Память* also favors a free-market economy and private property. What is more, Vasiliev revealed that he and other members abhorred Hitler for his racial theories but expressed sympathy for his fascist ideology.[32]

The alleged source of *Память*'s misfortune has been the "Ziono-Masonic plot" against Russia; they likewise condemn this plot as blameworthy for the disintegration of the economy, the denationalization of Russian culture, alcoholism, and ecological crisis. Further, *Память* charged Zionists with masterminding the revolutions, causing the deaths of millions over the course of the Russian Civil War, and inciting Stalin's personality cult. Within this movement's conspiratorial mind, the waning Soviet apparatus was supposed to be infiltrated by Zionists and Freemasons with the purpose of subordinating it to Jewish capital. The "Zionist Occupied Government" accusation has been a sound bite often proclaimed by *Память* personnel. Officially, however, the organization emphasized that its ideology was merely anti-Zionist and not

31 „About National-Patriotic Front 'Pamiat'," http://www.pamiat.ru/about.html (as of 20 April 2005).

32 John Dunlop, „A Conversation with Dmitrii Vasiliev, the Leader of Pamiat'," *Report on the USSR*, 15 December 1989, 13–15.

anti-Semitic. Through all of this, *The Protocols of the Elders of Zion* have been the most oft-quoted document in *Память* propaganda.

The doctrine of *Память* is, however, not without its contradictions: it clearly extols late Tsarist society, especially the figure of Nicholas II, while simultaneously glorifying Lenin. Within this paradigm, Lenin, out of no fault of his own, was surrounded by Jews and Freemasons, the most nefarious of which was Leon Trotsky. Like many right-wing extremists, *Память* sympathizers believe that many prominent Russian scholars, artists, and politicians have long been in league with Jews and Freemasons. As described by Stephen Carter, the society is likewise paradoxical concerning religion: "While many of its members are church-goers, there exists an anti-Christian element who regards the Christianization of Kievan Rus' as a Zionist plot designed to undermine the warrior-like qualities of the Slavs."[33]

Walter Laqueur presents a detailed picture of a customary *Память* convention:

> A typical Pamiat meeting would open with the ringing of church bells or the playing of patriotic marches. This would be followed by recitals from the works of patriotic writers past and present; on occasion a movie would be shown, highlighting some national monument or the beauties of northern Russia or of Siberia. There would be short speeches on subjects such as the systematic destruction of national monuments, above all in Moscow; the responsibility was put on 'Zionist' architects acting in close association with foreign Masonic enemies of Mother Russia.[34]

Within the last ten to fifteen years, *Память* has diminished in political influence and significance. Beginning in the 1989–1990 elections all *Память* candidates failed and became increasingly ostracized by others on the right. Though it still exists on some level, some historians are now viewing *Память* as a precursor—the first in a vast field that grew to be overcrowded. As the movement neglected to consolidate its platforms and form a cohesive political

---

33 Stephen Carter, *Russian Nationalism: Yesterday, Today, and Tomorrow* (New York: St. Martin's Press, 1990), 111.

34 Laqueur, *Black Hundred*, 207.

party with a resolute leader, it failed to meet the needs of post-Communist Russia. More specifically, *Память*'s ideology left too much room for interpretation and lacked a uniform practical application.

To be fair it must be emphasized that the faces of Russia's political right do not all necessarily subscribe to the racial ideologies of *Память* or past fantasies of the Black Hundreds. Indeed, liberals and moderately conservative nationalists dismiss them with disdain. Laqueur rightly clarifies: "How to draw the line between moderates and the extreme right? There is a simple rule of thumb. A basic difference exists between those who seek the cause of Russia's misfortunes entirely in the machinations and intrigues of foreign and domestic entities—and the others, who are willing to engage in introspection, self-criticism, and, where called for, penitence."[35] Laqueur draws with exactness the line distinguishing Solzhenitsyn from the extreme nationalist contingency in Russia. Likewise, Edward Ericson writes: "Far from fusing and confusing the two [*Память* and Solzhenitsyn] we should be emphasizing how far apart they are."[36] As will be discussed later, Solzhenitsyn first and foremost calls upon his countrymen for "repentance and self-limitation"; without this he does not believe Russia can be reborn and reach her national potential.

Solzhenitsyn's Unique Nationalism

By the late 1980s a chorus of right-wing Russian chauvinists were denouncing Western culture, economics, and politics on the same grounds as Solzhenitsyn, at least superficially speaking. What is more, there seems little doubt (as certain critics such as Aleksandr Ianov predicted) that the Russian extreme right expected the Nobel Laureate to make common cause with them. Such a presupposition, however, was deftly quashed by Solzhenitsyn in his 1990 publication of *Rebuilding Russia*, in which he outlined his vision for a renewed political apparatus in his country. It was clear in this piece that the author's disposition toward the Soviet Union clearly differentiated him from the camp of extreme national-patriots. Alla Latynina, a member of the editorial board of *Literaturnaia gazeta*, "speculated that Russian 'fundamen-

---

35 Ibid., xv.

36 Edward Ericson, *Solzhenitsyn and the Modern World*, 201.

talists' must have been seriously shaken by Solzhenitsyn's brochure, since in 'their crusade against Russophobes,' they had held Solzhenitsyn's portrait on their banners."[37]

It transpired that when the famous writer returned to his homeland in 1996, he was greeted by diatribe in the right-wing press. Eduard Limonov went on the offensive, stating "Aleksandr Solzhenitsyn is destructive for Russia."[38] Continuing this theme Aleksandr Prokhanov wrote: "He, in essence, was a major component of the Cold War and was used powerfully by opponents of the USSR. His contribution to the destruction of the Soviet Union and Communism was colossal"[39] (loss of the Soviet state was thought to be egregious by many extreme nationalists). Of course this invective would not be complete without a Zionist plot accusation attributed to Solzhenitsyn's dreams for the motherland. And indeed, Valerii Khatiushin was convinced that Solzhenitsyn was the most important of anti-Communist dissidents, the latter had allegedly begun his destruction of "the basis of government" with *One Day in the Life of Ivan Denisovich.*[40]

All things considered, how is one to conceptualize Solzhenitsyn's unique form of nationalism? Although the writer espouses special allegiance to his country and culture, he is in fact loath to be categorized as a "nationalist." Thus, if used, the term "nationalist" has to be defined with the utmost precision to avoid ambiguity. Given the aforementioned radical nationalist movements and the writer's intention to distance himself from them, it is certain that this concern of diction is more than an issue of semantics. Further, Solzhenitsyn knows perfectly well that with regard to Russia, the word "nationalist" rings with disparaging tenor, especially among international scholars. What is more, attribution of the word has proven for many years to be derisive ammunition in the hands of the writer's enemies. Edward Ericson said it well in writing: "The subject of Russian nationalism is a thicket; we must cut

---

37 John B. Dunlop, „Russian Reactions to Solzhenitsyn's Brochure," *Report on the USSR*, 14 December 1990, 3–8.

38 Eduard Limonov, „Aleksandr Solzhenitsyn razrushitelen dlya Rossii," *Knizhnoe Obozrenie* 23 (7 July 1994), 23.

39 Aleksandr Prokhanov, „Strasti po Solzhenitsynu," *Argumenty i facty* 25 (1994), 3.

40 Valerii Khatiushin, „Esli poimem—spasemsia," *Molodaya Gvardia* 3 (1995), 27–40.

our way through it patiently and methodically."[41] Let us make our way through this thicket to understand precisely what words such as "nationalism" and "nationalist" connote for Solzhenitsyn.

In a 1989 interview, David Aikman queried Solzhenitsyn directly: "Are you a Russian nationalist, and what does that mean for you?" The author's response:

> I am a patriot. I love my motherland. I want my country, which is sick, which for 70 years has been destroyed, and is on the very edge of death, I want it to come back to life. But this doesn't make me a nationalist. I don't want to limit anyone else. Every country has its own patriots who are concerned with its fate.[42]

He continues to deconstruct the word nationalist:

> Take the word 'nationalist'—it has become almost meaningless. It is used constantly. Everyone flings it around, but what is a nationalist? If someone suggests that his country should have a large army, conquer the countries which surround it, should go on expanding its empire, that sort of person is a nationalist. But if, on the contrary, I suggest that my country should free all the peoples it has conquered, should disband the army, should stop all aggressive actions—who am I? A nationalist! If you love England, what are you? A nationalist! And when are you not a nationalist? When you *hate* England, then you are not a nationalist.[43]

Undoubtedly, Solzhenitsyn possesses a deeply spiritual love for Russia. But according to his responses to queries on the subject, his sentiment has less to do with nationalism (especially considering this word's implication in the modern world) and more to do with patriotism. That said, the writer asserted in *The Mortal Danger* that the simple love of country, an inborn feeling

---

41 Edward Ericson, *Solzhenitsyn and the Modern World* (Washington, D.C.: Regnery Gateway, 1993), 116.

42 Aikman, „'Russia's Prophet in Exile,' Interview with Aleksandr Solzhenitsyn," *Time*, 134:4 (1989), 60.

43 Aleksandr Solzhenitsyn, *Warning to the West* (New York: Harper & Row, 1986), 107.

of patriotism, is today labeled "Russian nationalism." Notwithstanding, he defines patriotism in the following words:

> As we understand it patriotism means unqualified and unwavering love for the nation, which implies not uncritical eagerness to serve, not support for unjust claims, but frank assessment of its vices and sins, and penitence for them. . . . We ought to get used to the idea that no people is eternally great or eternally noble . . . that the greatness of a people is to be sought not in the blare of trumpets . . . but in the level of its inner development, in its breadth of soul.[44]

Thus a narrowly defined understanding of nationalism approaching a certain unworldly patriotism must be conceptualized if such a word is to be associated with Solzhenitsyn. With that definition in mind, let us proceed to associate the term "nationalist" or "nationalism" with Aleksandr Isaievich.

It is arguable that Solzhenitsyn, by virtue of his literary acclaim, is the most *internationally* notorious proponent of Russian nationalism. Surely this is true regarding Western perceptions of Russian nationalism during the final years of the Soviet Union and after its fall. Not only his animus toward the perceived materialism, secularism, and individualism of the West, but also Solzhenitsyn's contention of Marxism as a Western ideology have branded him the epithet of "Russian nationalist." But the Nobel Laureate is of a different order: one celebrating a type of Russian traditionalism, an idea which preserves a patriotism free of extreme right ideology. For example, scholars such as Leonard Schapiro claim that Solzhenitsyn is merely a realist, that his code of ethics is essentially benevolent and that his vision is progressive.[45] In that same camp, John Dunlop considers Solzhenitsyn to be a "liberal nationalist" so as to distinguish him from others to whom the nationalist label is usually attributed. In contrast, others, such as Andrei Siniavsky and Aleksandr Ianov, are wary of any nationalist hue for its proclivity towards right-wing authoritarianism and its probable political end—fascism. David Rowley

---

44 Aleksandr Solzhenitsyn, „Repentance and Self-Limitation in the Life of Nations," in Aleksandr Solzhenitsyn with Mikhail Agurskii et al. *From Under the Rubble*, trans. A. M. Brock et al. (Washington D.C.: Regnery, 1981), 120.

45 Leonard Schapiro, *Times Literary Supplement* 10 (November 1978), 1301.

attempts to describe Solzhenitsyn's unique form of nationalism, which the former believes is patriotic but not chauvinistic:

> What went unremarked in the debate over how liberal or authoritarian Solzhenitsyn was, was the fact that he stood for something unprecedented in Russian history. He has consistently advocated a Russia, by, of, and for Russians; he wants the Russian nation to be congruent with the Russian state. It is pre-eminently upon this point that Solzhenitsyn differs from the extreme chauvinist right wing. Extremists such as Zhirinovsky and Zyuganov, to choose only the most well-known representatives of those nostalgic for the Soviet state, should not be called 'nationalists' but 'imperialists'.[46]

An objective researcher will discover that the writer's nationalism borders on unique. Part of this is rooted in Solzhenitsyn's belief of the nation as a living, ethical entity. To be sure, his philosophy of nationhood transcends ethnic, linguistic, and cultural explanations of national identity. In the "Lichtenstein Address" he expounds on this, placing the highest value on the existence of the nation as not the ephemeral fruit of social formations but a complex, vivid, unrepeatable organism not invented by man.[47]

This is not to say that others have failed to write on the spiritual, metaphysical underpinnings of nationalism. Where Solzhenitsyn parts ways with many political thinkers is in his highly non-secular approach to nationhood. It seems evident that his ethos of nationhood diverges from certain civic, republican, creedal, and contractual foundations of nationhood at the heart of, for example, the American and French revolutionary experiences. Daniel Mahoney writes: "Solzhenitsyn criticizes all forms of nationalism that abstract from the properly penitential aspects of authentic patriotism. But if it is necessary to avoid Manichean judgments or one-sided national antipathies, it is

---

46 David Rowley, „Aleksandr Solzhenitsyn and Russian nationalism," *Journal of Contemporary History*, 32:3 (1997) 321.

47 Aleksandr Solzhenitsyn, „Lichtenstein Address," in *'The Russian Question' at the End of the Twentieth Century*, trans. Ermolai Solzhenitsyn (New York: Farrar, Straus and Giroux, 1995), 112–128.

also necessary to reject cool, scientific asceticism that tries to transcend the evaluation of national experience."[48]

It is also essential to point out that the writer's concept of "Russianness" is not simply an issue of blood. As Solzhenitsyn expressed in his 1995 publication *The Russian Question*, it is a matter of the spirit:

> We are justly reminded that on the expanses of the Russian plain, for centuries open to all migrations, a multitude of tribes blended with Russian ethnicity. But when we say 'nationality', we do not mean *blood*, but always a *spirit*, a *consciousness*, a person's orientation of preferences. Mixed blood does not determine anything. The Russian spirit and Russian culture have existed for centuries, and all those who feel themselves a part of this heritage in spirit, in consciousness, in heartfelt pain—are *Russians*.[49]

Solzhenitsyn further warns of extreme forms of nationalism, both among his own people and among the Jewish nation, citing the words of Russian philosopher Vladimir Solov'ëv:

> Доведенный до крайнего напряжения, национализм губит впавший в него народ, делая его врагом человечества, которое всегда окажется сильнее отдельного народа». Это высказано им в предупреждение националистам русским, но, хотя и глубоко расположенный к евреям, он в этой связи признаёт: «Утверждение своей исключительной миссии, обоготворение своей народности есть точка зрения древне-иудейская»[50]

Solzhenitsyn's advocacy of a Russian spiritual renaissance (the writer's own concept of nationalism) has explicitly and implicitly affronted some of his more ethnically sensitive readers—especially Jewish ones. Throughout the

---

48 Mahoney, *Solzhenitsyn: The Ascent From Ideology*, 110.

49 Aleksandr Solzhenitsyn, *'The Russian Question' At the End of the Twentieth Century*, trans. Yermolai Solzhenitsyn (New York: Farrar, Straus and Giroux: 1995), 102.

50 Vladimir Solov'ëv, *Natsional'nyi vopros v Rossii. Vypusk pervyi, 1838-1888, T.5* (Brussel: Fototipicheskoe vosproizvedenie, 1966), 13, 16.

history of Jewish Diaspora, outwardly expressed nationalism of a given host nation has often been associated with Jewish persecution. This connection is not entirely unfounded, however. In many cases of typical anti-Semitism, feelings of national pride have been conspicuously present. Almost the entire history of European Jewry bears witness of this—Russia being no exception. Nonetheless, Russophilia, with which Solzhenitsyn has been associated, does not necessarily connote anti-Semitism; on more than one occasion the writer has emphatically denounced those who believe that love of Russia and Orthodoxy equals anti-Semitism.[51] What is more, he has repeatedly made his support known for the state of Israel, a stance which many Jews consider the standard litmus test for determining or refuting anti-Semitism. Not only does the writer's endorsement of Israel appear culturally just, it bewilders critics convinced of his anti-Semitic nature. But even this is not enough to cleanse Solzhenitsyn entirely of the taint of bigotry.

According to Solzhenitsyn, the Orthodox religion with a bottom-up vertical line of local government (similar to that introduced by Tsar Aleksandr II in the 1860s) is the spirit of "nationhood" that collectively can redeem Russia from her current bondage, not too different from the classic triad "Orthodoxy, Autocracy, and Nationalism."[52] Furthermore, extreme forms of nationalism such as fascism, which can lead to likewise extreme anti-Semitism, seem to him (perhaps naively so) a highly unlikely scenario in Russia. The prerevolutionary Russia that Solzhenitsyn tends to romanticize was, at best, an era of great ambivalence towards the Jewish Question. In many respects the plight of Jews in Russian society has been an onerous one, arousing pity. In spite of this, the history of Russian transgression in pogroms and Jewish persecution is rarely mentioned by Solzhenitsyn in his novels or public statements. Lev Tolstoi has written that every writer has a sore point—Solzhenitsyn's was the suffering of his own people. He stated: "No country in the twentieth century has suffered like ours, which within its own borders has destroyed as many as seventy million people over and above those lost in the

---

51 E.g. Aleksandr Solzhenitsyn and Alexis Klimoff, *The Mortal Danger: How Misconceptions About Russia Imperil America* (New York: Harper & Row, 1980), 23-24.

52 Eduard Ponarin, „Aleksandr Solzhenitsyn as a Mirror of the Counter-Revolution," http://www.csis.org/ruseura/ponars/policymemos/pm_0150.pdf.

world wars—no one in modern history has experienced such destruction."[53] Further: "For my entire life, I have had the soil of my homeland under my feet; only *its* pain do I hear, only about *it* do I write."[54] Edward Ericson convincingly explains why Solzhenitsyn's sympathy for his own people cannot be equated with Russian chauvinism:

> Solzhenitsyn's Christian universalism eliminates any possibility of viewing one group of people as inherently superior to another. To be specific, it eliminates any possibility of his falling prey to Great Russian chauvinism—or, for that matter, to the anti-Semitism which it has sometimes spawned. He may feel especially sorry for Russia. He may devote his career to listening to the sad music of Russia and singing of it. But he cannot adopt the old myth of superiority of the Russian soul. The Russians may be a deeply religious people throughout their thousand-year-long history. But they are not a holy people, not in any such sense a chosen people. Solzhenitsyn does not claim as his own the concept of Holy Russia.[55]

Solzhenitsyn's form of nationalism reiterates that these feelings come in different shades and degrees and should not always be thought culturally elitist or chauvinist. For him such sentiments are much more rooted in spirituality than politics; they have everything to do with his land's history, Orthodox Christianity, and the ephemeral beauty of his country's expanse—it transcends state borders, being more a part of the metaphysical realm than of geographic demarcations. Solzhenitsyn's unashamed feelings for "Mother Russia" seem accurately interpreted by Rosette Lamont:

> Nationalism for this Russian novelist is not an idea, nor an intellectual fabrication, but an affective reaction, deeply rooted in the subconscious. It has something to do with the soil, the ever-changing scenery—the high mountains of the Caucasus, the wooded, gently hilly country

---

53 Solzhenitsyn, *From Under the Rubble*, 31–34.

54 *Solzhenitsyn: A Documentary Record*, Ed. Leopold Labedz (Baltimore: Penguin, 1972), 130.

55 Ericson, *Modern World*, 35.

around Voronezh, the spot where real Russia starts; it has everything to do with the people, particularly country folk, and their profound faith in God and in their saints; it is connected to the full bodied languages spoken in Georgia, Ukraine, Belorussia, and the dialects from the various sections of this immense land. Divorced from political ideologies, from the transient rule of inept tsars or ruthless bureaucratic dictators, Solzhenitsyn's nationalism is as natural as a tree, deeply rooted in the subsoil of a culture and rising toward the heavens in a desire to transcend the immediate situation.[56]

In his political essays Solzhenitsyn writes of his nation as a body, similar to the spirit of an individual, or—even on a religious plane—to the body of Christ. It is a nation that has suffered, is repenting, and now hopes to undergo rebirth, resurrection. He expresses Russia's contrition thus:

> We have become universally hated,
> Everywhere we shall be crucified,
> They will slaughter us on the Vistula,
> And in China build us funeral pyres.
>
> The Tartar's indelible birthmark
> And the foulness of Stalinist filth
> Have marked us all! Thrice cursed
> Will be Russia's name henceforth.[57]

Can this metaphorical national "body" be reconciled to non-Christian (not to mention non-Orthodox) peoples? Does Solzhenitsyn's vision for Russia allow for the existence of an historically dynamic ethno-religious group in a country that, in the mind of various types of nationalists, should be guided by the ethos of Christian Orthodoxy? These are difficult questions that can

---

56 Rosette Lamont, „Solzhenitsyn's Nationalism," in John Dunlop et al., *Aleksandr Solzhenitsyn: Critical Essays and Documentary Materials* (New York: Nordland Publishing, 1973), 95.

57 Scammel, *Solzhenitsyn*, 312.

fuel ethnic strife and even hatred when taken out of the writer's spiritual context.

VI The Jewish Question in Russian Literature

Anti-Semitism in literature is as old as Western culture. From Shakespeare to T.S. Elliot, the Jewish Question has appeared in literary narrative bearing witness to its social and historical significance for many generations. Russian literature is no exception. Indeed, the Jews of Russia have often alluded to a certain anti-Semitic tradition in Russian literature. To some this presents a quandary: whilst writers of Russia have notoriously defended humanitarian aims and ideals, many notorious names, from Pushkin to Chekhov, have portrayed Jews with stereotypically uncomplimentary, and periodically anti-Semitic, attributes. But other scholars, including Jews, find such accusations a gross generalization and not in touch with literary intent. Jewish writer Boris Goldman (under the pseudonym B. Gorev), in response to the anti-Semitic charge against the Russian literary heritage, writes:

> In such a general and categorical form this allegation is not correct, in any case one-sided and narrowly conceived, though containing a considerable grain of truth. Without any attempt to explain and analyze this phenomenon from a broad historical perspective, the authors of such assertions have played into the hands of hidebound Jewish nationalism and cast a false light on the beloved and, for Jewish democrats too, best traditions of Russian literature.[58]

In twentieth-century Russian literature Jewish characters have evolved into something new with a peculiar status. Poet and scholar Lev Losev claims that in Soviet literature even the typical "benign Jew" is derived from a "condescending, humiliating attitude" toward Jews.[59] Nobel Laureate Boris Pasternak (of Jewish decent) was unsettled by an excessive positive bias or sympathy to Jews, while other contemporary writers, Solzhenitsyn being no-

58 Boris Gorev , „Russian Literature and the Jews," *A History of Russian Jewish Literature*, (Ardis: Ann Arbor, 1979), 13.

59 Lev Losev, „Solzhenitsynskie Evrei," *Strelec* 1 (1989), 294–311.

toriously among them, have asserted their artistic license to depict nationalities as seems culturally ethical. Having said that, a difficulty arises: if a Jewish character is portrayed in a derogatory tone, can this be called a case of anti-Semitism, or simply a candid, ingenuous description of the world surrounding any writer? The copious points of view regarding Solzhenitsyn and the Jewish Question suggest the issue is perhaps not as fruitless as it may seem.

Contemporary Russian literature has cultivated several mythical Jewish images which reflect the various perceptions of reality and the social perspectives of those who participated in their creation.[60] Such mythical figures are embodied in merchant tradesmen, clever intellectuals and, towards the philo-Semitic end of the spectrum, pious rabbis, and simple family men, to name but a few key stereotypes. Many folkloric Jewish figures, like the merchant or clever intellectual, seem to serve as an antithesis to the Russian nation's idealized self identity—hence, a possible source of antipathy towards Jews. This "mythical Jew" appears as an inverted image of the idealized Russian—an epithet of Russian resistance to capitalism and perceived Jewish socialist aspirations.

Beyond the notion of a mythical Jew, however, there lurks literary anti-Semitism, which has long been a salient facet of the Russian literary tradition; in fact many Russian Jews believe their persecution to be an inexorable part of Russian culture. To assume otherwise would be for them to read with rose-colored lenses. Jewish poet Igor Guberman wrote:

Любой большой писатель русский
жалел сирот, больных и вдов,
слегка стыдясь, что это чувство
не исключает и жидов. [61] *

But making trite judgments of a writer's artistic worth on account of perceived anti-Semitic intent is unenlightening. Are we to condemn Shakespeare for his treatment of Shylock in *The Merchant of Venice*? Was Voltaire's writ-

---

60 Felix Dreizin, *The Russian Soul and the Jew: Essays in Literary Ethnocriticism* (Lanham: University Press of America, 1990), 1.

61 Igor' Guberman, *Gariki na kazhdyi den'* (Moskva: MP EMIA, 1992), 228.

* Citations are in Russian when no English translation is available or to uphold the artistic merit in certain poetry and prose excerpts.

ing in *Essai sur les moeurs* driven by overt prejudice towards Jews? Just as great Western writers have expressed similar ideas, Russian anti-Semitism in literature is multifaceted. At times it surfaces as a consequence of a nation's social climate, as opposed to being simply a result of one writer's ethnic bias or prejudice; it is born of Russian romanticism as well as xenophobia of foreign exploitation, competition, and individualism. Andrei Siniavsky (who, though not a Jew, deliberately used a Jewish pseudonym—Abram Terts) remarks in his "Literary Process in Russia":

> I would like to say something in defense of anti-Semitism in Russia. That is: what good is hidden, in the psychological sense, in the Russian unfriendliness (to put it mildly) toward the Jews? A Russian thinks it impossible that he may be the source of any evil, because deep in his soul he (probably like any other person) is good. He cannot believe that in the Russian state people are unhappy because of other Russian people or their own faults. A Russian is one of 'us'. One cannot be harmed by people of one's own kind; evil comes from aliens. Russian anti-Semitism is an alienation of evil.[62]

Among important Russian writers preceding Solzhenitsyn whose thoughts touched on the symbiotic relationship between Russians and Jews are Nikolai Gogol, Fyodor Dostoevsky, Anton Chekhov, and Boris Pasternak. Just as the politico-cultural history surrounding Jews and Russians must be understood in order to place Solzhenitsyn's Jewish Question into context, so must its legacy in the rich canon of Russian literature.

Gogol

Nikolai Gogol is among those who established the house of Russian literature. A Ukrainian-born writer, dramatist, satirist, and founder of critical realism *à la Russe*, Gogol is a revered name in literature. Throughout his prose the reader is dazzled by his imaginative power and linguistic mischievousness.

---

62 Abram Terts (Andrei Sinyavsky), „Literaturny protsess v Rossii," *Kontinent* 1 (1974), 183.

Perhaps Gogol's best known work is *Dead Souls*, seen by many as the first "modern" Russian novel.

Every neophyte writer in twentieth-century Russia became intimately familiar with Gogol; Solzhenitsyn's development no doubt included such immersion. In fact Aleksandr was called a "new Gogol" following the publication of *One Day in the Life of Ivan Denisovich*. Although Gogol does not include Jews profusely in his *oeuvre*, one encounters them at the forefront of an obscure early work: in his epic tale *Taras Bulba*, Gogol writes of Jews with pejorative strokes as well as subtle moments of sympathy.

What is uncanny but perhaps not uncharacteristic of Gogol's mysterious spirit is that *Taras Bulba* harmonizes very little with his other writing. Given this, what is the reader to conclude regarding Gogol's relationship with Jewry? Gogol achieved acclaim primarily for his satirical prose works; thus *Taras Bulba*, a narrative written in the spirit of Homer's *Iliad*, is a unique book in his canon. In fact, some critics suggest it may not have been written by him. Among such is Felix Dreizin, remarking: "Nothing in this analysis [his chapter on Gogol in *The Russian Soul and the Jew*] suggests that *Taras Bulba* is a work by Gogol—the man if not the artist."[63] Working for six years on the text, Gogol's *Taras Bulba* exhibited an apparently less tolerant attitude towards religion and perhaps a naive conviction of the virtues inherent in the "Russian Soul," a myth to which he made significant literary contributions.

Without a hint of Gogolian satire, the work is an exploration and glorification of the warrior Russian and Cossack spirit, containing outbursts of the crudest anti-Semitism and Russian chauvinism as well as its opposite—philosemitic sympathy. As an example of the former, consider the thoughts attributed to the Jew, Iankel: "The first thing that flashed through the Jew's mind were the two thousand gold ducats on Bulba's head, but he felt shame at his greed and struggled to stifle his eternal craving for gold which like a serpent encircles the soul of every Jew."[64] Indeed there are elements which appear unattributable to the author of this story—the pious Gogol who nearly joined a Christian monastery and even made a religious pilgrimage to Jerusalem. But this is the very essence of Gogol. With a writer this complex one must also see his grayness and ambiguity, not merely his potentially anti-

63 Dreizen, *Russian Soul and the Jew*, 10.

64 http://emotional-literacy-education.com/classic-books-online-a/taras10.htm.

Semitic color but also his work as an artistic depiction of ethnic strife in medieval Ukraine.

To illustrate, Gogol refers to Jews in his writing as *zhids* or *kikes*, as is the closest equivalent in English. In spite of this, the word *zhid* is not historically a demeaning term. Such linguistic neutrality is evident in the benevolent language found in *Taras Bulba* describing a dead Jewish woman lying in a street of the conquered Dubno:

> Looking about him, he perceived, on the farther side, a group of two or three men lying motionless on the ground. He fixed his eyes more intently on them, to see whether they were asleep or dead; and, at the same moment, stumbled over something lying at his feet. It was the dead body of a woman, a Jewess apparently. She appeared to be young, though it was scarcely discernible in her distorted and emaciated features. Upon her head was a red silk kerchief; two rows of pearls or pearl beads adorned the beads of her head-dress, from beneath which two long curls hung down upon her shriveled neck, with its tightly drawn veins.[65]

In the same work the term *evreika*, meaning "Hebrew woman," is also used, although it is not clear if Gogol used the words synonymously. Prior to and after Gogol's time, the borrowed word *zhid* assumed a neutral connotation as is seen in the works by the eighteenth-century writer Karamzin. In modern Russian, however, the term has assumed a highly offensive tone. For this very reason modern critics have translated the story's *zhid* as *evrei* in *Taras Bulba*, which rings without abuse to the ears of Jews. Also, in part due to this work, the Soviet Ukrainian Dictionary replaced *zhid* with *evrei*, so as to avoid amplification of anti-Semitism among modern readers interpreting the word in its modern context.[66]

The profuse circulation of *Taras Bulba* in the Tsarist and later the Soviet era historically encouraged militant Russian chauvinism, patriarchal order, and anti-Semitism. The more subtle Gogolian moments which potentially at-

---

65 Nikolai Gogol, *Taras Bulba*, trans. Peter Constantine (New York: Random House Publishing, 2003), 11.

66 Dreizen, *Russian Soul and the Jew*, 58.

tenuate rather than simply aggravate Judeo-Russian relations were likely not interpreted correctly through the filter of Soviet ideology. Indeed, such a tale, taken in the wrong context, augmented nationalistic proclamations dear to every Russian heart and inspired anti-Semitic ideas even if such was not the aim of the author. Further, *Taras Bulba*, in both its original and adapted versions, is rife with the idealized image of the "authentic Russian"—the archetype of which is so dear to Aleksandr Solzhenitsyn. For several generations, Russian children have learned by heart the following words from *Taras Bulba*:

> There have been comrades in other lands, too, but such comrades as in Russia there have never been. More than one of you has had occasion to be for a while in foreign lands; you see that there, too, are men! God's creatures, too, and you speak with them as with your own fellows; but when it comes to uttering a word from the heart—no! You see that they are clever people, but not the same; they are men like us but not the same! No, comrades, to love as the Russian heart can love—to love not with the mind or anything else, but with all that God has given you, all that is in you—Ah! . . . No one can love like that![67]

It is enlightening to juxtapose the treatment of Jews by Gogol and Solzhenitsyn respectively. The former's novel evokes a curiosity about the Jewish race: their idiosyncratic ways, their dress, and their exclusive, undying faith; Gogol's interest is derived from artistic investigation. On the other hand, Solzhenitsyn perceives the Jewish nation as a modern social issue as opposed to an aesthetic opportunity—this will be discussed in greater detail subsequently.

The character sketches in *Taras Bulba*, at least initially, suggest blatant antipathy towards Jews—the "mythical Jew" is painted as the antithesis of Russian magnanimity, courage, and heroism. What merely adds to the elusiveness of Gogol is that if the vociferous ideological proclamations of the novel are put aside, what is left has a droll, humane timbre; one wonders if Gogol's intention was as anti-Semitic as many modern readers suppose. Indeed, despite this evident Judeophobia in *Taras Bulba*, one senses authorial

---

[67] Gogol, *Taras Bulba*, 17.

sorrow for the plight of Jewry as well. Thus Gogol, like many other writers of Russia, is ambiguous with regard to Judaism. Whether or not the reader finds his work laden with prejudice, the writing of Nikolai Gogol shaped not only Russian nationalism but also Solzhenitsyn's understanding of the Jewish Question.

Dostoevsky

Fyodor Mikhailovich Dostoevsky is one of the preeminent writers of the modern age. Indeed, his literary art penetrated the psychology of man, the nature of morality, Christianity, and Western culture with feverish tales of contemporary Russian life. To illustrate his revered place in literature, lofty words such as "prophet" have come up when describing Dostoevsky. Such language has been cemented with Joseph Frank's Herculean biography of Dostoevsky entitled *Mantle of the Prophet*. In this spirit Solzhenitsyn has forged a link with Fyodor Mikhailovich, the former having achieved similar status with the profundity of his message and the sublimity of his language.

What often receives less attention when discussing Dostoevsky, however, are the anti-Semitic views threaded throughout his work. Until *The House of the Dead*, Jews were virtually nonexistent in Dostoevsky's writings, but beginning with this novel in 1862, the Jew assumed a place of growing consequence in his thought. For example, in the notorious essay "The Jewish Question," the author did not hide his anti-Semitism. But unlike Gogol, who in his native Ukraine had observed firsthand the antagonism between the Ukrainians and Jews, Dostoevsky had had little experience with Jews because there were so few living in St. Petersburg at the time. Eight years of military and penal servitude in Siberia, however, exposed Dostoevsky to both criminals and Jews alike. Like Solzhenitsyn, he emphasized the spiritual transformation of the individual more than social revolution.

A logical place to plumb Dostoevsky's outlook on Russian Jewry is in his diaries. For example, Biographer Joseph Frank asserts that the Jewish image in the writer's journal entries and correspondence can be expressed as "enemies of humanity."[68] His antipathy towards Jewry is derived from a belief that Jews are oppressors of the Russian people and generally cause suffering and misery. In his "official" pronouncements on the Jewish Question and in his artistic works Dostoevsky may have been inconsistent, but his private letters and diary entries exclude Jews from humanity. As Felix Dreizin wrote: "In the Dostoevskian world, anti-Semitism and humanism are perfectly compatible."[69]

Dostoevsky's attitude towards Jews is arguably less ambiguous than the common ambivalence prevalent in Russian literature. To be sure, he is more overt in expressing his distaste for Judaism. However, within Dostoevsky's universe one can search and even identify the writer giving credit where credit is due: He writes in "The Jewish Question" on the assimilated Jews "who ceased to share the prejudices of their nation:"

> I shall observe . . . that to all those gentlemen from among the 'top Jews' who are such staunch advocates of their nation, it is much too sinful to forget their forty-century-old Jehovah and to renounce him. And this is sinful not only because of national sentiment but likewise for other momentous reasons. And strangely: a Jew without God is somehow inconceivable; a Jew without God cannot be imagined.[70]

Some of Dostoevsky's most scathing material was written in *The Diary of a Writer*. Suspicious of any messianic doctrine other than that of Orthodox Christianity, he condemned the Jews as exploiters of his "humble countrymen" through usury, commerce, and inn keeping. Dostoevsky attacks Jews for their historical refusal of Christianity, which he feels places them outside the human family. Consider his letter dated 15 July 1880:

> The idea that those human races which receive some basic idea from their founders and following it exclusively through generations, must finally degenerate into something unlike the rest of humanity as a whole

---

68 Joseph Frank, „Foreword," in David Goldstein, *Dostoevsky and the Jews* (Austin: University of Texas Press, 1981), XI.

69 Dreizin, *Russian Soul and the Jew*, 65.

70 Fyodor Dostoevsky, *The Diary of a Writer*, trans. Boris Brasol (Salt Lake City: Peregrine Smith, Inc., 1979), 637.

> and even . . . into something hostile to humanity, as a whole—this is a true and deep idea. Such are the Jews from Abraham's time to ours, when they degenerated into Yids. Christ (apart from the rest of his significance) was a correction of this idea; he has broadened it to all-inclusive humaneness. But the Jews did not like the correction, they clung to the narrowness and straightforwardness, and so instead of humaneness they turned into the enemies of humanity, who reject everybody besides themselves.[71]

Further, he felt the Russian nation had a messianic purpose in the world. Such a notion found its most virulent expression in Dostoevsky's novel *Demons* where, in a conversation with Stavrogin, Shatov states:

> Reduce God to the attribute of nationality? . . . On the contrary, I elevate the nation to God. . . . The people is the body of God. Every nation is a nation only so long as it has its own particular God, excluding all other gods on earth without any possible reconciliation, so long as it believes that by its own God it will conquer and drive all other gods off the face of the earth. At least that's what all great nations have believed since the beginning of time, all those remarkable in any way, those standing in the vanguard of humanity. . . . The Jews lived solely in expectation of the true God, and they left this true God to the world. . . . A nation which loses faith is no longer a nation. But there is only one truth; consequently, only one nation can possess the true God. . . . The sole 'God bearing' nation is the Russian nation.[72]

In interpreting Dostoevsky's sentiments towards Jews, biographer Joseph Frank invented a new category for the writer—"the *guilty* anti-Semite." Against the backdrop of Dostoevsky's general xenophobia, however, his opprobrium for Jews may be considered relatively mild. Said Frank: "Dostoevsky was . . . unquestionably anti-Semitic, just as he was anti-French, anti-German, anti-English, and particularly, anti-Polish—indeed, anti-everybody

---

71 Fyodor Dostoevsky, *Complete Works in 30 Volumes*, vol. 30 (Leningrad: Nauka, 1972), 262.

72 Fyodor Dostoevsky, *Demons* (New York: A. A. Knopf, 1994), 265–266.

who was not Russian, and Great Russian at that. Dostoevsky's anti-Semitism . . . should be placed in this larger context of a more general xenophobia."[73]

Solzhenitsyn indeed derived great inspiration from the work of Dostoevsky, but it would be imprudent to assume that the former espoused the latter's extreme views of Jews. Dostoevsky's *Demons* documents the consequences of disrupting Orthodox Christianity and renouncing faith, particularly in the name of revolutionary socialism, thus producing an "existential chaos" which can be interpreted as anticipating both the Soviet encroachment on religion and the spiritual muddle of post-Soviet Russia. Ideological self-discovery appears as a persuasive attraction to individuals caught in such a situation. Dostoevsky speaks of the psychological situation which led to the great Marxist revolution in early twentieth-century Russia (long before that revolution took place). Further he scrupulously details the unsavory and nefarious nature of the characters driven to bring about such a revolution. This prescient work was certainly pondered by Solzhenitsyn in his research of the October Revolution and subsequent investigation of the Jewish role therein.

Chekhov

Among the pantheon of Russian writers, Anton Pavlovich Chekhov evokes a special luster, both at home and abroad. Many literary critics proclaim him Russia's (and perhaps the world's) foremost short-story writer. Indeed, he truly revolutionized the genre. What is more, among dramatists Anton Pavlovich has been hailed a modern-day Shakespeare. Although his last four titles (*The Seagull*, *The Three Sisters*, *Uncle Vania*, and *The Cherry Orchard*) contrast with conventional plays, they have become standard repertoire in the theatrical productions of many nations.

One paradox, seemingly contradictory to Chekhov's evident humanism and incongruous within itself, is his mysterious attitude vis-à-vis the Jewish Question. To be sure, much like Aleksandr Solzhenitsyn, there is dual evidence in the work of Chekhov evincing a truly ambivalent sentiment toward Jews. On the whole it is fair to say that the writer believed Jews who were

---

[73] Frank, „Foreword," in Goldstein, *Dostoevsky and the Jews*, XIII–XIV.

born and raised in Russia could never be truly Russian. Furthermore, Chekhov frequently categorized new acquaintances as *zhid* or *nezhid* (Jew or non-Jew); in letters it was not uncommon for him revert to derogatory language when speaking of Jews. To make Chekhov truly enigmatic, he fell in love with and was engaged to a Jewess. Likewise, one of Anton's dearest friends was a Jewish painter who greatly influenced the former's approach to his own art of writing.

Let us examine more deeply both sides of Chekhov's curious ambivalence toward Jews. Biographer Donald Rayfield suggests that, despite Anton's inherent contradictions and racial slurs, by nineteenth-century Southern Russian standards Chekhov was quite amicable towards Jews. Nowhere was this possible Judeophilia manifest more than in an indictment surrounding Alfred Dreyfus, which occurred whilst Chekhov was living abroad.

The "Dreyfus Affair" developed into a political scandal which caused a great stir in France for many years. It revolved around the 1894 treason charge of Alfred Dreyfus, a Jewish artillery officer in the French army. The Dreyfus Affair split France between the Dreyfusards (those supporting Alfred Dreyfus and implicitly against anti-Semitism) and the anti-Dreyfusards (those against him and against Jewish emancipation). As the Dreyfus case split the country, Chekhov, then in France, considered himself an ardent Dreyfusard. In taking such a position he nearly destroyed a relationship with his great patron, Alexei Suvorin, a conservative newspaper owner, by insisting on Dreyfus's innocence. To Chekhov's credit, Dreyfus was eventually exonerated because the conviction rested on false documents. Anton cited Voltaire's defense of Calas as an establishment of precedent during the affair.

Chekhov likened his affection for Jews unto his fondness for women—though no Jew in his view could truly assimilate into Russian culture, neither could a woman ever compete with a man intellectually; nevertheless he defended their civil rights with fervor. Yet as anyone who is familiar with his work knows, it is difficult to conclude what side of the coin this places Chekhov with regard to the Jewish Question. As with his philosophical, religious, and even artistic impulses, the writer is shrouded in mist.

Further exploration of Chekhov's filial and romantic relations with Jews reveals a curious episode taking place in 1886. During that year the playwright was apparently engaged to Dunia Efros, a young Jewish woman. This is entirely founded on a few letters Chekhov had written to friends, as well as some very formal notes in Dunia's hand. Interestingly enough, her name does not come up anywhere else by anyone else. What this means is also open to speculation. Indeed, her identity remains mysterious, and their engagement lasted less than six months at which point, as Chekhov remarked, "I broke with her, or rather say, she broke with me." This liaison inspired a play written shortly thereafter entitled *Ivanov*. Biographer Donald Rayfield illustrates how Chekhov's engagement and subsequent break-up with Miss Efros further deepens the writer's mysterious outlook on Russian Jewry:

> Dunia's Jewishness was certainly instrumental in bringing her and Anton together and then sundering them. Like many southern Russians, Anton admired and liked Jews. Always a defender of Jews, he asked Biblin why he used the word 'yid' three times in a one letter? Yet he himself used the word both neutrally and pejoratively and, like many southern Russians, Anton felt Jews to be a race apart with irredeemably unacceptable attitudes. 'Jew' and 'non-Jew' were categories in which he classified every acquaintance, even though utterances and his behavior make him, by the standards of the times, a judeophile.[74]

At times artists of different mediums cultivate friendships which foster greater understanding than that which is derived from the general public. In Chekhov's mind, musicians and painters tended to grasp more fully the essence of his work. The writer's friendship with and letters to artist Isaak Levitan adduce this. To be sure, the latter figure presents a relevant topic because Levitan, one of Russia's greatest landscape painters, was Jewish. The camaraderie between these two appears to have been mutually beneficial as well as a source of reciprocal inspiration. For example, Chekhov based his short story "The Grasshopper" on the real-life love affair between Levitan and Lika Mizinova, a young unmarried teacher who had for many years been an admirer of Chekhov. In the story the writer also bases a character called Dymov largely on himself, portrayed as a committed and disciplined worker who has no time for flippant romance. Likewise Anton found Isaak's work and aes-

74 Donald Rayfield, *Anton Chekhov; A Life* (New York: Henry Holt and Company, 1997), 124.

thetic philosophy to be of kindred spirit. A certain painting by Levitan entitled "The silent monastery," with the image of a monastery and planked bridges across a river, expressed deep reflections of the artist about life. It is known that this picture made strong impression on Chekhov. Moreover, Anton and Isaak lived through the worst period of political reaction in Russia in the 1880s when the slightest manifestation of free thought was stifled. Both had roamed the countryside near Chekhov's rented dacha at Babkino on the river Istra in the mid-1880s, and Anton would often travel to Levitan's country home to write whilst his Jewish friend captured the majestic Russian forestland in oil.

But Anton Chekhov's life and work also show a certain level of mistrust toward the Jewish race. The short story *Mire*, for example, appears to expose the writer's antipathy for Jews, if there is such, employing hackneyed anti-Semitic stereotypes. In the following passage the protagonist Sokolsky enters the home of Jewess Susanna Moiseievna and observes his surroundings. The prose is typically Chekhovian but, like Gogol's *Taras Bulba* and Solzhenitsyn's *Lenin in Zurich*, it reads with unexplainable prejudice towards Jews:

> There was scarcely anything in the room definitely Jewish, except, perhaps, a big picture of the meeting of Jacob and Esau. The lieutenant looked round about him, and, shrugging his shoulders, thought of his strange, new acquaintance, of her free-and-easy manners, and her way of talking. But then the door opened, and in the doorway appeared the lady herself, in a long black dress, so slim and tightly laced that her figure looked as though it had been turned in a lathe. Now the lieutenant saw not only the nose and eyes, but also a thin white face, a head black and as curly as lamb's-wool. She did not attract him, though she did not strike him as ugly. He had a prejudice against un-Russian face in general, and he considered, too, that the lady's white face, the whiteness of which for some reason suggested the cloying scent of jasmine, did not go well with her little black curls and thick eyebrows; that her nose and ears were astoundingly white, as though they belonged to a corpse, or

> had been molded out of transparent wax. When she smiled she showed pale gums as well her teeth, and he did not like that either.[75]

In the next passage Sokolsky comes to the estate of Mrs. Moiseievna to collect a debt. How to interpret Chekhov's depiction of Jewish lust for lucre is up to the reader:

> 'Here it is,' she said, picking out the key of the portfolio. 'Now, Mr. Creditor, trot out the IOU. What a silly thing money is really! How paltry it is, and yet how women love it! I am a Jewess, you know, to the marrow of my bones. I am passionately fond of Shmuls and lankels, but how I loathe that passion for gain in our Semitic blood. They hoard and they don't know what they are hoarding for. One ought to live and enjoy oneself, but they're afraid of spending an extra farthing. In that way I am more like an hussar than a Shmul. I don't like money to be kept long in one place. And altogether I fancy I'm not much like a Jewess. Does my accent give me away much, eh?'[76]

Objectively speaking these excerpts appear anti-Semitic. But as with the work of other writers who depict Jewish characters, Solzhenitsyn included, the author's intent is far from lucid.

Chekhov's appeal is reflected in many literary elements, but what is often suggested is the way he abstains from opining on issues of social morality and religious ethics, thus allowing readers to come to their own conclusions. But this presents a difficulty in plumbing the real feelings he had towards Jews. As is evident from his life, Chekhov, like many Russian writers, exhibited signs of both judephilia and anti-Semitism. This duality is emblematic of Russia's historical courtship with Judaism. Although quite different from one another artistically and philosophically, Chekhov and Solzhenitsyn both exhibit an apparent uncertainty or ambivalence towards Jewish place in the world.

---

75 Anton Chekhov, „Mire," http://www.ibiblio.org/eldritch/ac/mire.htm (as of 20 April 2005).

76 Ibid.

Pasternak

Russian poet Boris Pasternak was born into a renowned Jewish family in Moscow. His father, Leonid, was a professor at the Moscow School of Painting and his mother, Rosa Kaufman, was an acclaimed concert pianist. Their home was open to such guests as Rachmaninoff, Scriabin, Rilke, and Tolstoi. Pasternak's novel *Doctor Zhivago* was awarded the Nobel Prize for Literature in 1958, but he was compelled to decline the honor for political reasons. The novel itself was eventually banned in the Soviet Union and Pasternak was expelled from the Union of Soviet Writers. After *Doctor Zhivago* reached the West, it was soon translated into eighteen languages. Pasternak's name was rehabilitated posthumously in 1987, which made possible the publication of his major work in its original language.

Despite the Pasternak family's strong Jewish background, the Russian element of Boris's cultural *mélange* ultimately defined his person. To be sure, in contrast to the writers previously mentioned, Pasternak stands apart. He finds himself in the curious group of Jewish-born Russian poets, such as Osip Mandelshtam and Joseph Brodsky, who harbored misgivings about their ethnic heritage. In particular, Pasternak considered Zionism and cultural chauvinism to be a great scourge to Judaism. George Gibian wrote of the writer's ideological differences with his father, Leonid: "Boris Pasternak, we know from his friends' reports, did not share his father's pro-Zionist interpretations of the Jewish national character and his celebrations of Jewish spirituality."[77] Although he freely acknowledged his ethnicity, there was nothing more foreign to him than the display of Jewish nationalism and especially Zionism. Ronald Hingley describes Pasternak's sentiment during Stalin's anti-Semitic campaign: "Pasternak's racial origins were a sore point with him. He was not embarrassed to be a Jew, but he was at a loss what to do or say when it transpired that his Jewish descent was never forgotten or forgiven, despite the fact that he was 'in spirit a profoundly Russian poet.'"[78]

---

77 George Gibian, „Doctor Zhivago, Russia and Leonid Pasternak's Rembrandt," in John Garrard, ed., *The Russian Novel from Pushkin to Pasternak* (New Haven: Yale University Press, 1983), 206.

78 Ronald Hingley, *The Russian Mind* (New York: Charles Scribner's Sons, 1977), 171.

The highly acclaimed novel *Doctor Zhivago* was a means for Boris to deconstruct complex, ambivalent ideas vis-à-vis his Jewish background. In a letter to Olga Freidenberg, he writes of the new work: "In it I will square my accounts with Judaism."[79] It is the hero of the novel, Yurii Zhivago, who embodies the author's ideal Russian incarnation, exhibiting compassionate sympathy for the persecuted Jews. Juxtaposed against Yurii is the assimilated Jew Misha Gordon, showing frustration with modern Jewry, who likely mirrors Pasternak's own Jewish image. The amalgam of these two characters frames the writer's abstruse relationship with his ancestry. Consider the following dialogue between Yurii Zhivago and Misha Gordon from *Doctor Zhivago*:

> 'It's terrible,' said Yurii Andreievich when they were in sight of their own village. 'You can't imagine what the wretched Jewish population is going through in this war. The fighting happens to be in their Pale. And as if punitive taxation, the destruction of their property, and all their other sufferings were not enough, they are subjected to pogroms, insults, and accusations that they lack patriotism. And why should they be patriotic? Under enemy rule, they enjoy equal rights and we do nothing but persecute them. This hatred for them, the basis for it, is irrational. It is stimulated by the very things that should arouse sympathy—their poverty, their overcrowding, their weakness, and their inability to fight back. I can't understand it. It's like an inescapable fate.'

Gordon did not reply.[80]

Though Boris Pasternak was born a Jew, his estranged disposition towards Judaism prevented him from feeling any fear about the anti-cosmopolitan movement prevalent in Soviet Russia as the writer came of age. For Pasternak, the Jewish race was replete with cultural exclusiveness, which was expressed by Gordon in the same work:

---

79 Guy de Mallac, *Boris Pasternak: His Life and Art* (Norman: University of Oklahoma Press, 1981), 245.

80 Boris Pasternak, *Doctor Zhivago*, trans. Max Hayward and Manya Harari (London: Collins and Harvill, 1958), 118–119.

> Why didn't the intellectual leaders of the Jewish people ever go beyond facile *Weltschmerz* and ironical wisdom? Why have they not disbanded this army which keeps fighting and being massacred nobody knows for what? Why don't they say to them: Come to your senses, stop. Don't hold on to your identity. Don't stick together, disperse. Be with all the rest. You are the first and the best Christians in the world. You are the very thing against which you have been turned by the worst and weakest among you.[81]

As suggested by the above quote, Pasternak believed that assimilation was the answer to the Jewish Question. In his view, this implied the Jewish race uniting with the international community of Christians rather than clinging to an ancient ethnicity so often at odds with European statehood. He was convinced that national differences between Christians were arguably less significant: i.e. assimilation of Russian Jews rendered the Jew not Russian but simply Christian. Philosopher Isaiah Berlin wrote of Pasternak's affinity for assimilation: "This passionate, almost obsessive, desire to be thought a Russian writer with roots deep in Russian soil was particularly evident in his negative feelings towards his Jewish origins. He was unwilling to discuss the subject—he was embarrassed by it, but he disliked it; he wished the Jews to assimilate, to disappear as a people. . . . He spoke to me as a believing, if idiosyncratic, Christian. . . . If I mentioned Jews of Palestine, this, I observed, caused his visible distress."[82]

Historians are bewildered by Pasternak's uncanny ability to remain among the living whilst so many dissident writers fell under the sword of Stalin. Perhaps what is even more mysterious, however, is the apparent affinity Stalin had for Pasternak. Indeed Boris survived the anti-Semitic campaign not for his *bête-noir* of Zionism, but rather for Stalin's curious attitude toward him. For example, Pasternak refused to endorse letters condemning leading Soviet intellectuals and military leaders. Those defended by the writer included Mandelshtam, Tukhachevsky, Iakir, and others allegedly having committed high treason. In his characteristic *naiveté*, Pasternak wrote a letter to Stalin

81 Ibid., 122–123.

82 Isaiah Berlin, „Meetings with Russian Writers in 1945 and 1956," *Personal Impressions*, (New York: The Viking Press, 1980), 179–180.

outlining his motives for repudiating the denunciations. Countless people were summarily executed for lesser offenses.

Boris Pasternak's renunciation of the Nobel Prize in 1958 has always been treated with great clemency in the West: here was a man who refused to revile others, yet succumbed to the pressure to condemn himself. The poet was charmingly resilient to the duplicity of those friends who were coerced into acts and utterances of denunciation. The capacity for tolerance of this Jewish Russian was very different from what has been called the "moral self-indulgence" of Solzhenitsyn, who followed the progress of the Pasternak affair with remarkable frustration. His reaction to Pasternak's handling of the Nobel Prize was less than complimentary: "How could he flinch before the threat of exile and humbly plead with the government, mumbling about his mistakes and failings, about his 'own fault' as regards the novel, renouncing his own ideas, his very spirit?"[83] Rostropovich discloses Solzhenitsyn's feelings about Pasternak: "Such shameful, cowardly behaviour . . . those idiotic letters of renunciation Pasternak allowed himself to write!"[84] Pasternak's second wife, Ivinskaia, replied that Solzhenitsyn had had vocal support from friends and acquaintances but Pasternak, in contrast, had no prominent supporters. Ivinskaia noted the difference in the political atmosphere: "In those days it had been heroism merely to keep silence."[85] As with Pasternak, the Soviet government denounced Solzhenitsyn's Nobel Prize as a politically hostile act.

It is difficult to distil from Solzhenitsyn's writings the worth he placed on writers such as Pasternak—Jewish in race but Russian in spirit. Solzhenitsyn undeniably respected Pasternak, at least in the brotherhood of literary dissidence, but one wonders if Solzhenitsyn's above-mentioned diatribe against the poet reflected unresolved inner conflicts about Russian Jewry. In any case, the pioneering literary role of Pasternak's ideological disobedience to the Union of Soviet Writers paved a road for Solzhenitsyn to traverse his own battles against Communist ideology.

---

83 Christopher Barnes, *Boris Pasternak: A Literary Biography, Volume 2, 1928–1960* (Cambridge: Cambridge University Press, 1998), 375.

84 bid., 116.

85 bid.

VII The Critics respond to Solzhenitsyn's Jewish Character Sketches

Solzhenitsyn is given vigorous scrutiny by critics for his fictional characters—especially those of Jewish decent. Discussion regarding his alleged anti-Semitism appears to have begun with a 1972 publication in the *Jerusalem Post* by Mikhail Grobman, a Soviet émigré and fierce critic of the writer. However, Solzhenitsyn also had admirers among Jewish intellectuals defending him, including Mikhail Agursky and Roman Rutman, both of whom were Jewish dissidents still residing in the Soviet Union at the time. Later, in 1976, the London-based *Soviet Jewish Affairs* published a defense of Solzhenitsyn by Edith Frankel, an American writer, which was answered with allegations a year later by Soviet émigré Simon Markish. These initial articles, appearing shortly after the writer received the Nobel Prize, spawned the first public discussions concerning Solzhenitsyn and anti-Semitism.

Among Jewish critics already cited, Mark Perakh saw much to condemn in the writer's canon, beginning with an early play *The Love-girl and the Innocent.* The three Jews in the play—Arnold Gurvich, Boris Khomich, and Solomon the bookkeeper—were all of reprobate character, even blatantly corrupt and disgusting. Solomon, in Perakh's view, was depicted with excessively anti-Semitic strokes—those of a cunning, manipulative, corrupt Jew seeking control of the camp. Interestingly enough, of the three, Solomon was the only one based on a real person—Isaak Bershader, known to Solzhenitsyn at Kaluga Gate. Bershader was immortalized in volume III of *The Gulag Archipelago* as one of the despised camp elite allowed to choose mistresses from among the female camp members. Perakh's basic contention was that, in his works, Solzhenitsyn generally depicted Jews as villains and Russians as heroes. What is more, pejorative descriptions of singled-out individuals, even if historically accurate, created an overly generalized, untrue impression for the reader and thus were not a reflection of the reality of Russo-Jewish relations.

It would seem if Solzhenitsyn is not under enquiry for a derogatory representation of a Jew, then he is reproached for not including them at all.

Perakh further analyzed Solzhenitsyn's entire canon up to *Lenin in Zurich* and found fault in *One Day in the Life of Ivan Denisovich* for its exclusion of Jews. In his perception, the novella deliberately avoided the Jewish Question in spite of historically ubiquitous Gulag anti-Semitism, which in his mind should have been touched on by the author. It is not always clear why Solzhenitsyn makes the Jewish Question a more salient feature of a given novel and at other times does not. It seems the author did not want the theme to become overly-emphasized in novels where Jewish figures were present. Along the same lines, a criticism was made by Mikhail Grobman that *Cancer Ward* included no Jewish doctors and thus downplayed the role of Jewish physicians in Russian medicine. The very same novel was later condemned by ultra-conservative nationalist Ivan Samolvin, claiming *Cancer Ward*'s Lev Leonidovich, the "surgeon with hairy hands," an implicitly Jewish character in the story, exhibited Solzhenitsyn's philo-Semitism. The disparate interpretations of *Cancer Ward* make cogent assessments of Solzhenitsyn's Jewish Question hard to surmise. Likewise, according to Samolvin the protagonist's foil, Rusanov, unquestionably an ethnic Russian with such a surname, was the antagonist of the story. Although Solzhenitsyn never clearly states the chief surgeon Leonidovich's ethnicity, the character possesses many traits as well as psychological features common among Jews—namely irony, mockery, or wit. Lev Leonidovich is described thus in *Cancer Ward*: "In the simplest conversation, which had nothing funny about it, his usual expression was mockery, without any particular target."[86]

Many of Solzhenitsyn's readers express bemusement when he is accused of anti-Semitism. While some allegations can be attributed to Solzhenitsyn's display of Russophilia and nationalism, the majority of claims have come about as a result of specific Jewish character sketches in his historical novels, some of which have already been mentioned. As the writer's name began to assume great stature, especially following the Nobel Prize, certain critics began voicing opposition—no racist should win the Nobel Prize. Consequently, the author has been hounded since the 1970s for charges of anti-Semitism. It comes as no surprise therefore that with the publication of *Two Hundred Years Together*, a work dedicated to the Jewish Question, a new

[86] Aleksandr Solzhenitsyn, *Cancer Ward*, trans. Rebecca Frank (New York: Modern Library, 1983), 405.

round of anti-Semitic accusation is brewing, recalling past Jewish characters in early novels. Although Jews abound in the vast repertoire of Solzhenitsyn, some ignoble and others benevolent, considerable Jewish resentment has arisen for the treatment of Bogrov and Parvus.

Bogrov juxtaposed against Stolypin

Among controversial Jewish figures emanating from the pen of Aleksandr Solzhenitsyn is the personage Dmitry Bogrov, historical assassinator of Prime Minister Pyotr Stolypin in 1911. For the writer, Stolypin's murder was a pivotal turn in the history of Russia. Other historians, in contrast, claim that the Prime Minister was not as influential as the writer seeks to convey. The Tsar was not always benevolent toward Stolypin nor to his proposals, thus the latter's demotion was likely imminent even before his tragic end. In spite of this, Bogrov's story is given nearly a hundred pages of prose in *August 1914*. The importance of this Jew's appearance in the work, however, seems more a reflection of the stature of Bogrov's victim in the eyes of Solzhenitsyn.

In an interview with *Time* magazine in 1989, Solzhenitsyn likened the profound and seemingly unstoppable movement towards revolution in 1917 to a "gigantic cosmic wheel"—the "red wheel" of his epopee—in which everyone, including those who turn it, becomes a helpless atom.[87] Stolypin, for Solzhenitsyn, was the last tangible, political impediment to the revolutionary wheel. In the twilight of Tsar Nicholas II's reign, Stolypin was virtually the only figure seeming to know how to reform the political system of the Russian Empire. His detractors disdained him as a power-hungry, callous politician who was unscrupulous in pursuing his own career and who would use any means to restore the tsarist autocracy following the frightening turbulence of 1905. Stolypin's admirers, however, argue that he was a man of vision who pursued policies that would have transformed Russia into a modern state with social and political institutions comparable to those of the West. Although Stolypin did not eschew the use of force to extinguish unrest, he lamented bloodshed

87 Paul Gray, „Russia's Prophet in Exile: Aleksandr Solzhenitsyn publishes the first volume of his epic on the Bolshevik Revolution and gives a rare account of his life in Vermont. ('The Red Wheel') (interview)," *Time Magazine*, 134:4 (1989), 56–60.

and much preferred peaceful means to curb the opposition. In foreign affairs he was uncompromising in his insistence that Russia should avoid entanglements which could lead to military conflict. To be sure, he was deeply committed to monarchical rule, but he did not consider it advisable to eradicate the elected legislature or to deprive it of its authority. Solzhenitsyn is convinced that Stolypin's program, an amalgam of reformism, authoritarianism, and nationalism, was more likely than any other to lead Russia toward social and political stability. Unfortunately, Tsar Nicholas II, his followers, and ultra-conservatives would not relinquish a portion of their privileges and prerogatives in return for a reduced, albeit still significant, role in a changed Russia. They succeeded in undermining the Prime Minister's attempts at fundamental reform and thus scuttled Imperial Russia's last such attempt before its demise.

The figures of Stolypin and Bogrov in *August 1914* appear as foils; that is, every virtue of Stolypin seems counterbalanced by the respective vices of Bogrov. The latter is a complicated individual whose rich character development was undoubtedly given great forethought by the author. Bogrov is clever, witty, and possesses a disciplined mind capable of functioning systematically; further, he is attentive, vigilant, and determined. But he is also isolated and lonely. Bogrov is always in conflict and disagreement with those around him and prefers business-like dealings with people over friendship. Typical caricatured Jewish physical traits are attributed to him, such as piercing eyes and protracted lips. In addition, lack of masculinity seems a trait often given him by Solzhenitsyn in that Bogrov is slim, exhausted, squeamish, frail, and "cannot fall in love with any woman."[88]

Bogrov's depiction was brought under more scrutiny in 1984 by *Radio Liberty*. Lev Losev broadcasted a talk to the Soviet Union in which he analyzed the text in *August 1914* surrounding Bogrov and, specifically, the psychological implications for the author. He observes that one of the defining aspects of *August 1914* is the "Russian national character." In contrast, Bogrov is spiritually "rootless," a "cosmopolitan," having nothing remotely Russian in his blood. Such a parallel is unlikely due to chance because Solzhenitsyn emphasizes the theme of Jewish nationalism in Bogrov's history.

---

88 Aleksandr Solzhenitsyn, *August 1914*, trans. M. Glenny (New York: Bantam, 1974), 117.

The "historical Jew" (Bogrov) is the murderer of Stolypin. In Solzhenitsyn's eyes, Bogrov's impropriety is less important than his being a Jew.[89] In response, D. M. Thomas discusses the Lev Losev and *Radio Liberty* criticisms of the Nobel Laureate:

> Radio Liberty Staff member Lev Roitman declared the program's 'propaganda of hatred' an insult to any decent person. It would have led hundreds of thousands of Jewish listeners in the Soviet Union to an 'odious conclusion.' The program's producer, Georg V. Schlippe, just as angrily demanded an apology from the accusers. Professor Losev, a pen name for Lifschutz, responded with dignity, pointing out that he himself was a Russian Jew, and had tried only to analyze Solzhenitsyn's attitudes and imagery. He had studied the text very carefully, and come to the conclusion that, while the snake imagery has sometimes been used by anti-Semites, Solzhenitsyn intended the snake to represent rationalism. The conflict was philosophical, not racial. Losev expressed the hope, as a Russian Jewish writer and concerned American citizen, that their 'high-pitched insults and threats' would not succeed in getting their real target, the novelist, banned from their transmitters.[90]

Certain readers and critics feel Solzhenitsyn overstated Bogrov's Jewish motive in murdering Stolypin. Others, moreover, have been disquieted by Solzhenitsyn's overall treatment of Bogrov, claiming emphasis on the latter's ethnicity exposes the author's "clandestine" anti-Semitic design, blaming Jews for Russia's collapse into Communist oblivion. Historian Richard Pipes criticized Solzhenitsyn's apparent overemphasis of Bogrov's Jewish ethnicity thus:

> When dealing with the assassination of his hero Peter Stolypin by Dmitry Bogrov (whom he named 'Mordka' or Mordechai, lest anyone miss his nationality), Solzhenitsyn attributed to the assassin, without any historical warrant, a desire to prevent Stolypin from reforming Rus-

89 Lev Losev, „Velikoe Budushchee," *Kontinent* 42 (1984), 315.

90 D. M. Thomas, *Alexander Solzhenitsyn; A Century in His Life* (New York: St. Martin's Press, 1998), 490–491.

sia, since what was good for Russia was bad for the Jews. In fact, Bogrov came from a thoroughly assimilated family—his grandfather was a convert and his father a member of the Kievan Nobles' Club—and he had no Jewish interests in mind.[91]

There is, however, disagreement regarding Professor Pipes's interpretation of the history in question. Contrary to a belief that Bogrov came from a Russified family which rescinded Judaism, Alexander Klimoff counters that Bogrov's grandfather, although converting to Orthodoxy at one point, reconverted to Judaism after 1905. Young Dmitry was urged to convert to Orthodoxy in order to further his law career but vehemently rejected the notion, feeling a connection to his nationality. Although Pipes believes otherwise, the nickname Mordko was not attributed to Bogrov by Solzhenitsyn to emphasize the former's Jewishness. Mordechai was in fact the first name showing up in Bogrov's birth certificate, although he went by "Dmitry." As Klimoff writes: "Solzhenitsyn is solidly in tune with the sources when he depicts him (Bogrov) as a pathological product of the revolutionary subculture."[92]

Besides Alexander Klimoff, other scholars have come to the defense of Solzhenitsyn, pointing out that accusations, such as those concerning Dmitry Bogrov, do profound injustice to the writer. Advocates of Solzhenitysn have included Michael Agursky, Mstislav Rostropovich, Adam Ulam, Robert Conquest, Vladislav Krasnov, Lev Losev, and Elie Wiesel. The latter, a Jewish survivor of Auschwitz and acclaimed author of *Night*, explained his reasons for exonerating Solzhenitsyn: "He is too intelligent, too honest, too courageous, too great a writer. For Solzhenitsyn to be an anti-Semite would be wholly out of character. I am only disturbed by what seems to be an unconscious insensitivity to Jewish suffering."[93]

Unfortunately the author's emphatic denials of anti-Semitism go routinely unheard or ignored. On repeated accounts Solzhenitsyn has publicly refuted any anti-Semitic feeling and even mocked anti-Judaic fixations of the

---

91 Richard Pipes, „Solzhenitsyn and the Jews, Revisited," http:www.benadorassociates.com/article/141.

92 Alexis Klimoff, 'Re: AIS & the Jews,' Solzhenitsyn-1 472 [email discussion list] (5 April 2003) <solzhenitsyn-1@yahoogroups.com>.

93 Elie Wiesel, as quoted in D. M. Thomas, *Alexander Solzhenitsyn; A Century in His Life* (New York: St. Martin's Press, 1998), 491.

Russian political right, citing honorable Jewish figures in his prose and speaking of his own amicable relationships with Jewish friends and colleagues. It is at least arguable that the analysis of Bogrov in *August 1914* is actually more accurate than some would care to admit. Solzhenitsyn gives a balanced survey of Bogrov's life and aspirations, making mention of his bravery and moments of heroism, even if he suggests that such were misguided. Aiming at objective historicity in his novel, the author draws on reputable accounts of the man's life including memoirs of Bogrov's own brother and of former revolutionaries, especially those of Egor Lazarev. These accounts provide evidence that Solzhenitsyn's portrayal of an emotionally unstable Bogrov was not inaccurate, nor was attributing to the latter's torment over the plight of Russian Jews a motive to oust Stolypin.

Solzhenitsyn hypothesizes that Bogrov labeled Stolypin an anti-Semite not for his overt curtailment of Jewish rights, but for his intention to preserve the Russian character of the state. Bogrov's inner monologue contemplates the Jewish Question on the eve of revolution in *August 1914*:

> Some might say that Stolypin had introduced no anti-Jewish measures. No, but he had created the general atmosphere of depression. It was under Stolypin, and with the election of his Third Duma, that the Jews had begun to give in to despondency, to despair of ever obtaining the right to exist as normal human beings in Russia. Stolypin had done nothing directly against the Jews, he had even made lives easier in some ways, but it did not come from the heart. To decide whether or not a man is the enemy of the Jews you must look below the surface. Stolypin boosted Russian national interests too blatantly and too insistently—The Russianness of the Duma as a representative body, the Russianness of the state. He was trying to build not a country in which all were free, but a nationalist monarchy. So that the future of the Jews in Russia was not affected by his goodwill towards them. The development of the country along the Stolypin lines promised no golden age for the Jews.[94]

[94] Solzhenitsyn, *August 1914*, 462.

Though Solzhenitsyn may have over-emphasized Bogrov's "Jewish" motive in murdering Stolypin, the balance of *The Red Wheel* suggests no ascription of guilt to the Jewish nation by the writer. He makes clear the shortsightedness of the regime at the time which, as much as anything else, was responsible for the leftist tendencies of many Jewish intellectuals in early twentieth-century Russia.

Parvus as a Personification of Evil

Perhaps the quintessentially sinister character sketch of a Jew by Solzhenitsyn is that of Israel Lazarevich Helphand, or simply Parvus, in *Lenin in Zurich*. In this pre-published chapter of *The Red Wheel* the writer stages Lenin's encounter with Parvus during the former's Swiss exile. As the Great War wreaks havoc throughout Europe and Russia begins to sustain great losses, Lenin is left to advocate revolution in Switzerland. In spite of this, he is not prepared to get involved in the unpleasant business of provoking revolution at all, but fancies pondering on Marxist theory and reading European newspapers in the hope that the war will both lead to the destruction of the Tsarist system and bring about a more widespread European revolution. Lenin recognizes his own torpor and hopes that someone or something will come along to jostle him out of it, but does not act to break the impasse. In his dialogue with Parvus, the latter is trying to persuade Lenin to release his underground Russian forces for his own plotted revolution, financed by Germany. For it to come to fruition the wealthy Jewish revolutionary is counting on the powerful Leninist underground in Russia. Parvus cannot fathom why Lenin is reluctant to join him and uses all of his skills to persuade Lenin. Critics, however, see in this episode a demonstration of Parvus's essentially negative Jewish character traits. What Lenin does not disclose to Parvus as he stonewalls is that there is no Russian underground. All Lenin has at this time is a small group of bovine Swiss leftists. Yet, in his favor, instinct or circumstance causes him to turn down Parvus's offer to help him return to Russia, incite revolution with German financial leverage, and recognize the importance of the removal of the Tsar and the establishment of the Provisional Government once these events have occurred.

It should be mentioned that the prose depicting Lenin's encounter with Parvus is fictitious—the meeting described in *Lenin in Zurich* never took place. Solzhenitsyn, in his research of Bolshevik history, sought to establish a connection between the two to show that part of Russia's 1917 downfall can be attributed to foreign machinations, in this case via the German government. Lenin is actually described as hallucinating the entire visit and dialogue with Parvus. The latter is described in a dream in the following lines:

> Snap. The suitcase had burst open . . . and freeing his elbows, straightening his back, he unfolded, rose to his full height and girth, in his cramped legs, came one step, two steps closer. There he stood, life sized, in the flesh, with his ungovernable belly, the elongated dome of his head, the fleshy bulldog features, the little imperial—looking at Lenin with pale watchful eyes. Amicably as ever.[95]

Solzhenitsyn dispenses with all subtlety as he continues the description of Parvus: "How shamelessly Parvus displayed his wealth even in little things . . . and on his visits to Zurich he stayed in the most expensive hotel, Bauer au Lac. In Bern he ambled about a cheap student canteen (dinner, 65 rappen) in search of Lenin, puffing the most expensive cigars."[96] Even if these descriptions were accurate, one can almost hear the distant cries of affronted readers wondering why their great literary beacon would resort to such overtly pejorative Jewish stereotypes. Solzhenitsyn correctly portrays Parvus cajoling Lenin to accept German financial support for the Russian Revolution, but he takes a further fictional liberty: his description of Parvus appears to be without one redeeming feature. In the account, this surly character has been expelled from the party for misappropriation of funds, profiteering, and chasing after "bosomy blondes" in public.

Solzhenitsyn goes beyond generally repulsive traits such as debauchery and gluttony, however, to attribute slimy, demonic qualities which normally are only employed by the most ardent of Jew haters. Rancour-Laferrière rightly comments that "many of Parvus's traits seem to have come

95 Aleksandr Solzhenitsyn, *Lenin in Zurich*, trans. Harry Willets (New York: Farar, Straus and Giroux, 1976), 128.

96 Ibid., 115.

straight out of an anti-Semitic catalogue."[97] Yet more intriguing is the manner in which Solzhenitsyn stages the deal or proposition made by Parvus to Lenin, which seems to echo a symbolic "deal with the devil" of sorts. Parvus leans over Lenin urging him, breathing upon him marshy breath, even accidentally dripping "behemoth blood" onto the latter's hands: "But Parvus's hippopotamus blood spurted from the letter into Lenin's feverish hands, poured into his veins, swirled threateningly in his bloodstream. To prevent it from rising above his elbows, Lenin dropped the letter on the table as though it were heavy and flopped down helplessly in the chair."[98] Not only does the hackneyed stereotype of inherent lust for lucre and the typical contradiction of "coincidental capitalist-cum-international communist" shine through in this decadent character, but unabashedly vile character traits make up Parvus's person.

Transitioning from the insidious to the blatantly lascivious, the drama of the next scene envisions the two upon a bed. Interpretations of this fiction have been made alluding to homosexual lechery as the impetus of revolution. Thus a devilish collusion is suggested involving a demonic Jew and Lenin, himself partially Jewish. It seems possible that Solzhenitsyn envisaged Lenin engaged in a pact with a demonic figure of sorts. In considering the implications of this prose on Lenin and Parvus it is important to remember that there is a Russian tradition of interpreting political events through the medium of literary creation. Such is the case in *The Red Wheel* wherein the scrupulously researched facts are mingled with literary and artistic license.[99]

According to Mark Perakh, "Solzhenitsyn felt no hesitation in stimulating anti-Semitic feeling" in his treatment of Parvus.[100] Indeed, if Solzhenitsyn truly harbors anti-Semitic feelings, they have contributed to his descriptions of Parvus. Historically the Marxist millionaire Israel Lazarevich Helphland (1867–1924), or Parvus, did play a role in financially fomenting the Russian revolution. The imagery of "behemoth blood" pumped into Lenin's veins appears to represent German money poured into Russia. Evidence accumu-

---

97 Daniel Rancour-Laferrière, *Russian Literature and Psychoanalysis* (Amsterdam: John Benjamins Publishing, 1989), 146.

98 Solzhenitsyn, *Lenin in Zurich*, 116.

99 Carter, *Russian Nationalism* , 65.

100 Mark Perakh, „Solzhenitsyn and the Jews," *Midstream*, 23:6 (1977), 15; Sidney Monas, „Gulag points west," *Slavic Review*, 40:3 (1981), 462.

lated by Zeman and Scharlu (*The Merchant of the Revolution*) asserts that Parvus and his supporters did in fact transfer large sums of money from Germany to the Bolsheviks in Russia during the First World War.[101] In spite of the partial truths surrounding the character of Parvus in *Lenin in Zurich*, it is difficult to justify Solzhenitsyn's explicitly dark character sketch of this man and his part in revolutionary history.

Benevolent Jewish Characters

To extract Solzhenitsyn's underlying view of Jews in Russian history, the reader must expand his or her own vision of history and literature looking beyond characters such as Bogrov and Parvus. Gentiles (non-Jews) exist in his books weighed down by the same malevolent attributes, but an obvious bias in nearly all of the criticism is that the claims are often derived solely from negative evidence. Unfortunately, the benign depictions of Jews within the author's canon are rarely addressed by critics.

Consider, for example, Major Adam Veniaminovich Roitman, an assimilated Jew from the novel *The First Circle*. This individual is characterized not solely by his Jewish surname but through inferential moments. The author never directly calls Roitman a Jew but mentions that he is visited by an old friend who is "also Jewish." Although toiling to be a part of the Soviet dream, Roitman is presented as an upright man, good to his Gentile wife, and said to be liked by the prisoners because he is a "decent human being." Interestingly enough, the author dedicates several pages to this man's nocturnal contemplation on the evils of anti-Semitism:

> The Jews were in favor of the Revolution that had rid them of pogroms, of settlement restrictions. And now, imperceptibly, Iosif Stalin, hiding behind a screen of second rank figures, was grasping the whip of the persecutor of Israelites. When a group of people is hounded because they exploited others, or have been members of a dominant caste, or hold certain political views or have certain acquaintances, there are al-

101 Joel Carmichael, „German Money and Bolshevik Honour," *Encounter* (1974), 81–90.

> ways reasonable (or pseudo-reasonable) grounds for taking action against them. At least one would know he had chosen his lot for himself, that he could have chosen otherwise. But nationality?[102]

Here Solzhenitsyn touches on the immorality of persecuting any nationality, in this case the Jewish one. But perhaps he goes further in empathizing with the Jewish Roitman. Rancour-Laferrière considers this to be a moment of the writer's identification with the Jewish nation as a suffering race: "I would add that, at the moment of writing them (lines dedicated to Roitman) Solzhenitsyn was not an anti-Semite of any kind, but a Judeophile."[103]

Further, from the same novel, Lev Grigorevich Rubin should not be overlooked. This character is based on a long-time Jewish friend of Solzhenitsyn, Lev Kopelev, a Russian-born Jewish writer and human rights activist who was imprisoned in a Soviet labor camp after he objected to Soviet troops' brutality against German civilians in occupied territory following World War II. Kopelev's memoirs corroborate much of what was attributed by Solzhenitsyn to the character Rubin. Like Roitman, Rubin was also dedicated to the Communist movement, but the writer is sympathetic in his treatment of him and seems to possess empathetic understanding of Rubin's lot in life: "They persecuted him, not caring that each such conflict destroyed him and brought him closer to the grave."[104] In life, Solzhenitsyn's friendship with Lev Kopelev continued beyond the prison years, the latter helping bring about the publication of *One Day in the Life of Ivan Denisovich* and remonstrating against Solzhenitsyn's expulsion from the Soviet Union.

Perhaps most favorably drawn is Ilia Isakovich Arkhangorodsky in *August 1914*. This character represents the cultural mélange of Jew-cum-Russian patriot loyal to the Tsar. Solzhenitsyn describes his involvement in milling in Rostov-na-Donu during the revolutionary years. Like Rubin, Arkhangorodsky also has a basis in biographical history; apparently such a man lived in Aleksandr's hometown and was a good friend of the author's family, looking after his mother following the revolution.[105] Ilia is a respected engineer

---

102 Aleksandr Solzhenitsyn, *The First Circle* (New York: Harper & Row, 1968), 489.
103 Rancour-Laferrière, *Russian Literature and Psychoanalysis*, 156.
104 Solzhenitsyn, *The First Circle*, 476.
105 Scammell, *Solzhenitsyn*, 47–48.

and entrepreneur, a practical man, a builder of Russia. Wise restraint is attributed to him in his views of Russia's political reality. Solzhenitsyn paints him as a philosopher of sorts, possessing some of the traits of a mythical Jewish rabbi. Although a Jew, he harbors zealous Russian patriotism. Says Akhangorodsky:

> The process of history is much more complex than you, with your crude plans to lay violent hands on it, can imagine. The country one lives in is in trouble. So which is right to say, 'Go to hell, I'll have none of you,' or to say, 'I want to help you, I belong here?' Living in this country, one must make up one's mind once and for all and stick to one's decision. Do I really belong to it heart and soul? Or don't I? If I don't, then I can smash it or leave it, it makes no difference which I do. . . . But if I *do* belong to it, then I must adapt myself to the slow process of history, by work, by persuasion and gradual change.[106]

Arkhangorodsky is an assimilated Jew. His wife celebrates both the Passover and Easter. Similar in his disenchantment with things Jewish to the revered Pasternak, Arkhangorodsky despises the traditional Jewish occupations of merchant or usurer. In all, this character was carefully polished and, though a Jew, has scarcely anything stereotypically Jewish about him. Perhaps this "assimilated" Russian Jew was the ideal evolution for such individuals in Solzhenitsyn's mind and consequently such a character is sketched in shining colors. For critics convinced of Solzhenitsyn's "true" anti-Semitic nature, such a benevolent Jewish character is confusing. One of Solzhenitsyn's more dedicated Jewish critics, Mark Perakh, admitted Arkhangorodsky is "extremely attractive."[107] Generally speaking, Solzhenitsyn's admiring critics agree that Arkhangorodsky approaches the writer's real feelings towards Russian Jews.

It should not be overlooked that Solzhenitsyn's world of prose oscillates between literature and history. Indeed, the relationship between the two is subtle. What is more, it can be found in each of the writer's works, but the proximity to one or the other polarity varies from book to book. Edward Eric-

106 Solzhenitsyn, *August 1914*, 670–671.
107 Perakh, „Solzhenitsyn and the Jews," 13.

son writes: "Perhaps the most helpful way to view this subject is to see all his major works as literary, with the two poles of his literary field being fiction and history. . . . Solzhenitsyn's works can be placed on a continuum from the more fictional and less historical to the less fictional and more historical. . . . At one end is *Candle in the Wind*; while at the other is *The Gulag Archipelago*."[108]

In Solzhenitsyn's prose one will ultimately find that Jews are portrayed as most individuals are in real life—possessing both virtue and vice as anyone else. There is not a clear sign of overall sympathy or hostility towards the Jewish race when the characters are taken as a whole.

[108] Edward Ericson, *Solzhenitsyn; The Moral Vision* (Grand Rapids: William B. Eerdmans Publishing Company, 1980), 117.

VIII The Political Jewish Question in Post-Soviet Russia

In 1989 an unprecedented 71,000 Soviet Jews were granted exodus from the USSR; of these only 12,117 immigrated to Israel. Since the Soviet Union's collapse, however, over one million Russian Jews have emigrated to Israel. In the interim, democratization in Russia has been accompanied by a considerable degree of unfortunate irony for the country's remaining minorities, especially the Jewish stratum. The disappearance of Soviet-era repression exposed Jews who remained to a resurgence of anti-Semitism, encouraged by ultra-nationalist groups as well as racist demagogues such as Vladimir Zhirinovsky (who is, ironically, himself half-Jewish). Nonetheless, there has not been a return to mass anti-Semitic incidents in Russia or elsewhere throughout the former Soviet Union.[109]

Solzhenitsyn's latest writing in *Two Hundred Years Together* promotes awareness of the modern, post-Soviet Jewish Question. Given the ephemeral, and at times contradictory features of Russia, the situation for Jews is highly complex. To speak of it is to proceed on "along the edge of a knife," says Aleksandr Solzhenitsyn:

> История «еврейского вопроса» в России (и только ли в России?) в первую очередь богата. Писать о ней — значит услышать самому новые голоса и донести их до читателя. (В этой книге еврейские голоса прозвучат много обильнее, нежели русские.) Но, по порывам общественного воздуха, — получается чаще: как идти по лезвию ножа. С двух сторон ощущаешь на себе возможные, невозможные и ещё нарастающие упрёки и обвинения.Чувство же, которое ведёт меня сквозь книгу о 200-летней совместной жизни русского и еврейского народов, — это поиск всех точек единого пони-

109 „History of the Jews in Russia and the Soviet Union," *Wikipedia Free Encyclopedia* http://en.wikipedia.org/wiki/History_of_the_Jews_in_Russia_and_the_Soviet_Union (as of 20 April 2005).

мания и всех возможных путей в будущее, очищенных от горечи прошлого.[110]

During *perestroika* and in the early years following the Soviet collapse, the Russian press openly discoursed on many social ills, including anti-Semitism. This new era of great social metamorphosis marked the emergence of nationalist and dissident groups, with which Solzhenitsyn's name has become associated, although the writer does not necessarily express open sympathy for such movements. Jewish scholar Theodore Friedgut claims that, in addition to Russian nationalist groups, a section of the intelligentsia centered in sundry literary unions of the Russian Federation began publishing voluminous accusations against Jews as despoilers of Russian culture and pernicious seekers of world domination in the familiar spirit of *The Protocols of the Elders of Zion*.[111] From this point of view, Russian Jews were beginning a new cycle of their tragic, historical role as "scapegoats" for a presupposed loss of national identity and culture unsettling to ethnic Russians. With the new freedoms ushered in by *glasnost'*, however, a more strident opposition to anti-Semitism emerged from a newly-public Jewish press; not to mention non-Jews whose ideology rejected national hatred and xenophobia, promoting ethnic tolerance as an ethos fundamental to Russia's future.

Periodically the Jewish social reality can be lost in the dust that flew with the fall of the Communist regime, but it becomes ever more visible as that dust settles and new symbiotic social identities take shape in the Russian state. To address this issue, both anti-Semitism derived from the state and that which exists at a grassroots level must be considered. Some Jews, including Iakov Etinger, feel that there is no more state-sponsored anti-Semitism in Russia today, such as existed at different times during the Soviet era. Dr. Etinger finds that the greater part of the Russian population rejects persecution of Jews and claims this is supported by polls revealing a marginal 5–8% still harboring anti-Semitic sentiments.[112]

---

110 Aleksandr Solzhenitsyn, *Dvesti let vmeste 1795–1995, chast' II* (Moskva: Russky Put,' 2002), 5.

111 Theodore Friedgut, „Antisemitism and Its Opponents in the Russian Press: From Perestroika until the Present," http://sicsa.huji.ac.il/3fried.htm.

112 Yakov Etinger, „Is There a 'Jewish Question' in Russia?," http://www.jewishpost.com/jp0610/jpn0610t.htm.

For some, however, this is a saccharine perception of modern Russian society. Other Jews feel that overt persecution is manifest in everyday life. Evgeny Satanovsky, President of the Russian Jewish Congress, remarks *apropos* the level of anti-Semitism in post-Soviet Russia: "I would not say it is institutionalized on the state level. The elite is what matters, and the Russian elite is not on the caveman level of consciousness anymore. There is mundane distrust of Jews in every country every day. Where there are no Jews, someone will inevitably be suspected of being one. Not only Jews are affected however. That goes for all ethnic groups. They all are distrustful of others to some degree or the other."[113] It is arguable that both prior to and after the October Revolution there has existed a type of "traditional" anti-Semitism that rises to the surface given a demand for scapegoats.

Jewish persecution, however, is taking a new shape within post-Communist Russia. Soviet-era maltreatment of Jews was for many an accepted part of life, profoundly affecting the post-WWII generation. Because anti-Semitism was perhaps a subtle element of party ideology and propaganda, it proved counter-productive among many Russian intellectuals who rejected prejudice in the same manner that they rejected Communist ideology. Perhaps the inclusion of anti-Semitic rhetoric in the undertone of former Soviet ideology can in turn be attributed to the ambivalent status of Jews in the early post-Soviet years: the Jewish people have always been associated with capitalism and the West—ideals many Russians perceive as a model for their economic future. But the Utopian vision of capitalist prosperity was nearly destroyed with the collapse of the ruble in August 1998 and, unfortunately, many Russians seek to place the blame on Jews. In fact, belief in former Soviet propaganda which decried Jews is now being cultivated, catalyzing renewed anti-Semitism. Although Soviet ideology ostensibly combated anti-Semitism, such persecution was fostered in actual practice.

Post-Soviet anti-Semitism is exhibited in various media forms. From racial slurs on the street to destruction of Jewish edifices, ethnic persecution is alive and well in the new Russia. In many cities it is not out of the ordinary to see swastikas and anti-Jewish slogans spray-painted on buildings and gravestones. As in other countries, extremist hate groups such as the Black Hun-

113 Vremya Novostei, „An Interview with Evgeny Satanovsky, President of the Russian Jewish Congress," *Johnson's Russia List*, 21 January 2002.

dred have found efficacy in the internet to disseminate anti-Jewish literature in Russia. *Mein Kampf* as well as other foreign anti-Semitic literature is readily available, no doubt a result of confusing nationalism with racial prejudice. To combat the crimes spurred by such malevolent influence, Russian justice is ill-equipped, and government figures—who commonly express concern to specific groups of local Jews or Western countries demanding Russia take more steps to curb acts of bigotry—do little to generate public condemnation. Hence, the current political setting in Russia is far from ideal for making explicit statements against acts of anti-Semitism.

The persecution against Jews in present-day Russia has been expressed in three main ways.[114] The first, which is relevant to Aleksandr Solzhenitsyn, is also likely the most rife. It is embodied in Russophilia and Slavophilia—the expression of anti-Semitism as a result of perceived diminution of Russo-Slavonic cultural identity. Within this mentality the Russian national character is held to possess a unique cultural mission in the world conveyed predominantly in Eastern Orthodox Christianity, the traditional village community, and the rich geographical expanse of Eurasia. This variety of anti-Semite often celebrates Russian messianism—the belief that Russia alone preserves Christianity in its purity by virtue of Moscow (the Third Rome) and the sixteenth- and seventeenth-century myths of "Holy Rus'," the land of the "ever suffering" Russian people. Popular in the 1970s and among present-day Russian nationalists, this messianism may be found in the works of the founding fathers of Russian nationalism; in nineteenth-century literature, in particular Pushkin and Dostoevsky; and especially in the twentieth century by Solzhenitsyn, who is thought to romanticize past eras of Russian history. Historically, these Slavophile philosophies took root during the eighteenth and nineteenth centuries in the wake of burgeoning industrialization and influential Western democracy which gradually found intellectually fertile soil in Russia. It is not uncommon for Slavophile rhetoric to disparage the Jews, who are thought of as non-assimilating, manipulative, exclusive, and power-hungry. More importantly, Jews are perceived as a race implanted into Russia and, given their propensity for individual profit and prosperity, they have been looked upon with opprobrium by Slavophile Russians.

---

114 Friedgut, „Anti-Semitism and Its Opponents in the Russian Press."

A second form of anti-Semitic expression in Russia fits perfectly into the template of anti-Zionism. This group contests Zionism solely as a political ideology but disclaims any general racial discrimination against Jews. Since anti-Zionism is considered political in nature rather than racial, it can seem justified in the eyes of many. From the time of its emergence in the nineteenth century as a Jewish movement, Zionism has provoked opposition from not only outside the Jewish community, but also from within. This is due to the ambiguous ethnic identity among Jews as a single nation dispersed throughout the world and the continuing unstable existence of Israel as a state. From the perspective of Russian anti-Semites, Zionism is seen not as a movement for the establishment of Israel, but as an international conspiracy striving for world domination. It is no wonder then that this is the group that will not lay to rest the myth of *The Protocols of the Elders of Zion*. Thus every Russian Jew, whether sympathetic to Zionism or not, is liable to be profiled by wary anti-Zionists fearful of hostile Jewish power draining the lifeblood of Russia. Where the "national" anti-Semites interpret Jewish presence as erosion of Russian culture, "international" anti-Semites warn of Jewish dangers to the entire world.

The third group of anti-Semites and perhaps the most extreme is called the "zoological" anti-Semite. The Jew, wherever he may be, is considered an insidious, malign individual, and always a foreigner. This prejudice is no doubt interwoven with theories of international Jewish collusion, but the main idea emphasizes the individual Jew as an innate personification of degeneracy. In effect this group is a derivative of fanatical Christian anti-Semitism, viewing Jews as both collectively and individually culpable in the rejection of Christ. Friedgut further describes this group:

> The zoological anti-Semites remain an isolated lunatic fringe, few but vociferous, and dangerous as a simplistic answer to the pent-up frustrations of a disoriented and disgruntled public. For the liberal Russian intelligentsia, this group is perhaps the most difficult with which to deal. Their accusations of blood libel, ritual murder, and satanic conspiracy are echoed not only by the ignorant, but by supposed intellectuals on the pages of literary journals. To combat such vestiges of medieval su-

perstition with rational discourse often appears as frustrating as sweeping back the tide with a broom.[115]

Most would agree that Solzhenitsyn cannot be associated with these latter extreme forms of Jewish vilification. While he calls for Jewish acknowledgement of atrocities committed on Russian soil, such pleas are for the mutual healing and continued symbiosis of the two ethnicities.

To reach a balanced understanding of Russo-Jewish cultural instability one must first understand but then look beyond Tsarist discrimination, anti-Zionism, and Soviet glass ceilings imposed on Jews in the Communist era. It is equally essential to understand the present state of Russia and the role (or perceived role) played by the Jewish social stratum amidst the social bedlam of democratic consolidation. It seems, aside from the aforementioned "tradition" of anti-Semitism, that there are two fundamental variables shaping contemporary Russian anti-Semitism. Firstly, Jewish intellectuals played a conspicuous role during the preliminary phases of *perestroika*, which lamentably spelled poverty for the bulk of the Russian population. The second factor is more significant with respect to everyday manifestations of anti-Semitism, but is also derived from the first: Jews are prominent among the so called "oligarchs" presently controlling plentiful key sectors of the economy, joint ventures, and banks.

The New Oligarchy

The new usage of the term *oligarchy* departs from the traditional Russian meaning of the word. In Russian, at least before 1997, *oligarchy* referred to the official power of a minority ruling elite. A dictionary edited by Vladimir Dahl, for example, defined *oligarchy* as "a form of rule, where power rests in the hands of a small group of elite oligarchs."[116] This definition corresponds to the interpretations of Plato and Aristotle, who were the first to identify the oligarchic form of rule. For these Greek thinkers, oligarchy was a state structure

---

115 Ibid.

116 Vladimir Pribylovsky, „Oligarchs, True and False," http://www.jamestown.org/publications_details.php?volume_id=16&&issue_id=624.

where the right to occupy a state position was confined to those with property. To the extent that these are always in a minority, their government was ruled by the few (from the Greek *oligos* - few). A characteristic of oligarchy would be rule for the benefit of private interests, and not the general will. In contemporary Russian journalism, however, *oligarchy* is taken to mean unofficial power, that is, plutocrats who, from behind the scenes, pull the strings of presidents, premiers, ministers, and governors. A century ago a shadow government of this sort was called the "financial oligarchy," a term first used by a French author under the pseudonym Lysis. The concept was picked up by the Austrian economist Rudolf Hilferding, and by Vladimir Lenin. It is worth mentioning that Aleksandr Solzhenitsyn was first to attribute the term *oligarchy* to the new generation of plutocrats reaping astonishing wealth in Russia's political transition.[117] To quote the writer's own words: "Nothing resembling democracy currently exists in Russia. The country is ruled with impunity by a vertical axis leading from the president and the government, while its economy is controlled by a stable and closed oligarchy of 150 to 200 ex-Communist apparatchiks and New Russians, who amassed instant fortunes through banditry."[118] It seems that when Solzhenitsyn called the Eltsin government an oligarchy, he had in mind the Aristotelian meaning of the term—a small group of officials functioning as a collective Eltsin.

The profits of the oligarchy are immeasurably higher than the revenues of the majority of the population. The names of leading oligarchs—Berezovsky, Gusinsky, Khodorkovsky, Smolensky, Fridman, Abramovich, and Mamut—are in effect familiar to all Russians, since many oligarchs are hoping to play a political role in the country and tend to intervene—often unwisely—on domestic issues. Consequently, they provoke significantly negative responses in Russian society. Although there is no dearth of Armenians, Azeris, Tatars, or even ethnic Russians among big businessmen, a part of the Russian population regrettably focuses on the Jews. Solzhenitsyn was critical of President Putin's decree of immunity given to former President Eltsin, whom the writer feels should appear before court to answer not only for his

---

117 Daniel Mahoney, „Aleksandr Solzhenitsyn and the Moral Foundations of Democracy," http://www.assumption.edu/news/mag/assumagsp00/Mahoney.html.

118 Pribylovsky, „Oligarchs, True and False."

own behavior as president but also for that of the oligarchs and all who have exploited the turmoil of the country to enrich themselves illegally.

With the same virulence he displayed in haranguing the Soviet regime, Solzhenitsyn has been attacking the nascent post-Soviet Russian government ever since its genesis. In his view a spiritually stunted kleptocracy arose after 1991 in his homeland wearing the visages of Eltsin, Chubais, and later Putin, to name a few (although Solzhenitsyn later expressed approval to Putin for his "efforts in healing the nation"). He reserved some of his harshest invective, however, for the oligarchs, who have proposed to change Russian law to allow the free sale of agricultural land, nationalized since 1917. Solzhenitsyn warns that these individuals are buying and will continue to buy up land at bargain basement prices with the fortunes they have stolen, leaving many Russians landless. Concerning the post-Soviet economic measures, Solzhenitsyn is quoted: "Privatization has meant that our valuable national companies have been given away for 1 to 2 percent of their actual worth. Nobody tells us whether the stolen 98 percent will ever be returned or if it is already lying somewhere in a foreign bank."[119] No doubt Solzhenitsyn realizes that Jews account for only a portion of the "kleptocracy"; he has never made statements to imply the contrary.

Unfortunately, as stated above, there is evidence that the Russian populace tends to give credence to the belief of a "Jewish oligarchy" and further associates slander of the oligarchs with defending Russia from Jewish exploitation. Solzhenitsyn is periodically accused of espousing similar opinions by those waiting to blow the anti-Semitic whistle at any political whim. Although his caustic language should not be interpreted as anti-Semitic—given the climate of current Russian economic hardship wherein many citizens harbor discriminatory feelings towards the oligarchs (especially those of Jewish ethnicity)—misperceptions abound and unfounded accusations can easily be mounted.

The current Russian government has expressed public condemnation of anti-Semitism and displays a desire to assuage the unconstructive rhetoric surrounding the Jewish Question in Russia. Vladimir Putin has on more than one occasion spoken out against anti-Semitism along with all forms of xeno-

119 „Solzhenitsyn: Russia Rooted in Rot," http://www.newsmax.com/articles/?a=2000/5/14/172120.

phobia and racial hatred. The Russian President further expressed remorse that many Jews are leaving the land of their birth and stressed the exigency of discouraging Jewish emigration from Russian soil. What may seem astonishing to certain Jews is that Solzhenitsyn, despite being defamed as an anti-Semite, shares this sentiment with the Russian President in regretting the Jewish flight from Russia, which commenced in the 1970s and continues to the present day. He claims this is yet more proof that Jews and Russians still have not learned to live together. Jews, he writes, have never felt at home in Russia, even when revolution removed the barriers they faced. While being a proponent of the state of Israel, he is skeptical of Zionism as a motivation for emigration, writing: "Soviet Jews who were able to emigrate loudly cried: Let my people go! That was an incomplete quote. In the Bible it reads: Let my people go, so that they may worship me in the desert (Exodus 5:1). But somehow, many of those let go went not to the desert, but to bountiful America."[120]

120 Solzhenitsyn quoted by Sam Greene, „Fatal Heritage," http://www.tol.cz/look/CER/article.tpl?IdLanguage=1&IdPublication=14&NrIssue=46&NrSection=1&NrArticle=9083&ALStart=30.

IX *Евреи в СССР и в будущей России*

What fuels the fire of Solzhenitsyn's disputed anti-Semitism has been the publication of a nearly forty-year-old essay entitled *Евреи в СССР и в будущей России* (*Jews in the USSR and in Future Russia)* allegedly written in the mid-1960s but not published until 2001. The article has not yet been translated into English nor has it received considerable attention in the press. A further complication is that Solzhenitsyn condemns the work's publication, though he has not categorically refuted authorship. Nevertheless it deserves analysis and sheds further light on the Jewish Question as it is perceived both by Solzhenitsyn and, symbolically, Russia.

As we shall see, the idea for a piece dedicated to the Jews of Russia likely became a reality in the 1960s. Solzhenitsyn and his first wife, Natalia Reshetovskaia, frequently visited the home of Professor Nikolai Kobozev, whose wife was Jewish. In Kobozev's impressive library, Solzhenitsyn spent hours reading the copious titles dedicated to the Jewish Question. At this time he reportedly composed the essay which became *Jews in the USSR and in Future Russia* and received leave from the estate to keep it in the library. Much later, in the late 1980s, the son of the late Professor Kobozev unexpectedly offered to sell the article by Solzhenitsyn, which was being kept in the library to the writer's by then ex-wife Reshetovskaia. It is not clear what his motives were in selling such a socially charged document, but disdain for Solzhenitsyn has not been ruled out. Reshetovskaia had not known of the article's existence at the time, but agreed to buy the work and subsequently submitted it to be preserved in the "secret writings" section (отдел секретных рукописей) of the Pushkin House.[121] In some unknown way the article slipped out of the Pushkin House and fell into the hands of Anatoly Sidorchenko who published *Jews in the USSR and in Future Russia* in 2001, just following the release of the first tome of *Two Hundred Years Together.* Con-

121 Natalya Reshetovskaia quoted by Valery Kazhdaya, „Opus-68, ili vypadenie iz predelov tsivilizovannogo polya," www.e-slovo.ru/152/opus.htm.

cerning the article's unexpected and unendorsed publication, Aleksandr Solzhenitsyn expressed bemused wrath. He wrote:

> Это хулиганская выходка психически больного человека. В свою пакостную желтую книжицу он рядом с собственными «окололитературными» упражнениями влепил опус под моим именем. Ситуация настолько вываливается за пределы цивилизованного поля, что исключается какой бы то ни было комментарий, а от судебной ответственности этого субъекта спасает только инвалидность.[122]

The "subject" of which the writer is speaking is Sidorchenko. In 1967 the latter graduated with honors from the Leningrad University Faculty of Philosophy and, four years later, was awarded a Doctoral Degree from Moscow State University. However, for his highly unorthodox philosophical views on Bolshevism he was admitted to the Serbsky Secure Psychiatric Hospital. He was thought to be suffering from "clinical Judeophobia," of which the author *Jews in the USSR and Future Russia* is also accused. Consequently, Solzhenitsyn's emphatic condemnation of the publication led many to disbelieve the allegations of his authorship.

More questions were raised when the announced publication date of the second volume of *Two Hundred Years Together*—November 2002—came and went with no sign of the second volume in bookstores until 2003. But this was not an occurrence of great alarm; Solzhenitsyn's novels had been delayed in the past. The delay might very well have been to stimulate discussion of one and the same book, but Solzhenitsyn perhaps also created distance between the volumes to leave room to assess the readership's response and subsequently make amendments and revisions. However, there was also speculation that publication had been delayed because of the 1966 essay's sudden appearance. How the writer responded to the publication of his alleged early work following the release of the first volume is difficult to determine and remains speculative. Enemies of Solzhenitsyn claim that he delayed his book's release in order to change the manuscript and distance it from the more incendiary essay of his past. This does not completely add up,

---

122 „Solzhenitsyn: Interview with the Moscow News," *Moscow News* 25, 19–25 June 2001.

however, because it is clear that Solzhenitsyn left certain parts unchanged. For example, part 5 of *Jews in the USSR and in Future Russia* is rewritten nearly word for word in *Two Hundred Years Together* Part II. Consider the following extracts, first from the latter:

> Что Бог избрал для своего человеческого воплощения и, во всяком случае, для исходной проповеди именно *эту* нацию и уже потому она *избранная* — этого не может отрицать христианин. «Распни, распни Его!» — то было всеобычное неизбежное ожесточение всякой тёмной фанатичной толпы против своего светлого пророка, — мы же всегда помним: Христос пришёл почему-то к евреям, хотя рядом были ясноумые эллины, а подальше и всевластные римляне. Эту загадку религиозной избранности — как не признать.[123]

And then juxtapose with the former:

> Что Бог избрал для своего челевеческого воплощения именно эту нацию и потому она в самом деле избранная—от этого никуда не деться во всяком случае христианам. Не водить, что "нашего Христа распяли," такие-сякие—то было обычное ожесточение всякой фанатичной толпы против своего пророка—но вспомнить: а Христос-то их избрал почему-то, хотя рядом были ясноумные эллины. Эту загадку избранности—признать и принять.[124]

To be impartial in this analysis one must appreciate the fact that there is real controversy over Solzhenitsyn's authorship of the article. He has never officially acknowledged writing it and reacted with considerable astonishment at its publication. In his response to the press Solzhenitsyn used words such as "falsification" and "forgery" to describe the pamphlet. In spite of this, he does call the work a *chernovik* (rough draft). Solzhenitsyn expresses his fiery discontent with the Moscow *Komsomol* which published an article on the alleged essay:

---

123 Solzhenitsyn, *Dvesti let vmeste*, 18.

124 'Aleksandr Solzhenitsyn,' *Evrei v SSSR i v budushei Rossii*, (Slaviansk: Pechatnyi dvor, 2000), 19.

> Впаривает мне выражения типа 'ленинско-еврейская революция.' Смеет обсуждать воровскую публикацию – с её сквозным хулиганским изгажением и грязной фальсификацией – выкраденных моих черновиков 40-летней давности. Ему вторит Эхо ... Отвечаю я – за свою книгу, а не за то, как её потрошат и выворачивают.[125]

Solzhenitsyn further explains how these forgeries appeared and concludes:

> И остаётся догадываться почему же вдруг оживились и гебистские фальшивки 70-х годов, и клевета на лагерные годы мои с 40-х на 50-е, и годы войны, и юности, - почему на всё это дружно кинулись и за океаном и у нас – именно с начала 2003 года?....Новые нападчики не брезгуют ни какой подделкой. Самые старые, негодные, не сработавшие нигде в мире и давно откинутые фальшивки, методически разработанные и слепенные против меня в КГБ за всю 30-летнюю травлю,- приобрели новую жизнь в новых руках.[126]

Despite the strong language used by Solzhenitsyn to condemn the publication, this 1960s work does seem in many respects to be the early predecessor of *Two Hundred Years Together*, albeit a more forthright glimpse into the author's mind and perhaps a less delicate interpretation of Russo-Jewish history. As is apparent upon first reading, it would seem to be an uncensored view of Russian Jews in the fiery language of Solzhenitsyn's earlier years. Consider phrases on the source of anti-Semitism such as: "В возникновении антисемитизма евреи виноваты сами, что причины антисемитизма лежат в свойствах самого еврейского народа."[127] And further as the article speaks candidly of Jews' dual loyalty and citizenship:

> Трудность в том, что ни в ту, ни в другую сторону до конца сдвигнуть этого вопроса нельзя: большинство евреев и не уедет в Изра-

---

125 „Aleksandr Solzhenitsyn obvinil svoikh kritikov v klevete," http://lenta.ru/culture/2003/10/20/Solzhenitsyn.

126 Ibid.

127 'Solzhenitsyn,' *Evrei v SSSR i v budushei Rossii*, 10.

иль (когда отпадут нелепые глупые нынешние ограничения) и не ассимилируются до конца (это для них—национальное самоубийство!)—остаться непременно среди нас, но постоянно помня о своём двойном подданстве, двойной лояльности.[128]

Israel Shamir writes that if the 1960s pamphlet was a passionate harangue of a procurator, then *Two Hundred Years Together* is the judicial conclusion which interprets history more objectively.[129]

The reader must remember that if *Jews in the USSR and Future Russia* is the work of Solzhenitsyn, it is not likely within the thread of thought he espouses currently—the writer has the right to change or develop his opinion over the course of 40 years. As is apparent in the above quote, Solzhenitsyn expressed vehement disapproval at the appearance of the 1966 piece and threatened legal action against those that acted without his blessing. In spite of this (and aside from the fact that the article is written in the majestic style of *The Gulag Archipelago*, which Sidorchenko could not duplicate), the publication of *Two Hundred Years Together* Part II leaves little doubt of *Jews in the USSR and Future Russia*'s authorship. Significant parts of the latter work, including quotes from Pamerants, are integral parts of both. But Solzhenitsyn has not definitively denied authorship of the document and consequently has opened himself up to media storms.

---

128 Ibid., 68.

129 Israel Shamir, „Evreskie Ruchi v Russkom More," http://www.zavtra.ru/cgi/veil/data/denlit/083/32.html.

X *Двести лет вместе*

In 1991 David Remnick remarked, “One only wishes that Solzhenitsyn himself would put the matter to rest by taking a firm and public stand against anti-Semitism instead of making a few passing remarks in interviews.”[130] For many scholars and readers alike, Solzhenitsyn has answered this request with his latest work.

In 2001 the writer published the *editio princeps* of *Двести лет вместе (Two Hundred Years Together)*, followed by the second volume in 2003. The decision to brave the perilous waters of Judeo-Russian relations in no less than a two-volume historical work shocked many in literary and socio-historical circles. The writer is advanced in age and, consequently, this exposition will be among his last literary offerings to the world. Surely Solzhenitsyn is aware of this fact and hopes readers will share in his entreaty for Judeo-Russian healing.

As an historical account, *Two Hundred Years Together* is sympathetic towards the Jews, though far from uncritical. One of the main themes is a plea for improved understanding and mutual empathy between the two nationalities. In the prologue Solzhenitsyn writes: “Автор понимает свою конечную задачу так: посильно разглядеть для будущего взаимодоступные и добрые пути русско-еврейских отношений.”[131] Ultimately he holds that the “truth” encompassing Russo-Jewish relations is morally vital to both nationalities. Many Jews applaud this benign intention, but the book also makes clear that certain Jews played a vanguard role in the rise of Soviet Communism, earning the appellation “yeast of the Revolution.” Such a statement is unpalatable to many regardless of matters of historical veracity. Paying his characteristic minimal attention to critics, Solzhenitsyn thought the time auspicious to open up what he calls a “necessary subject,” especially considering the mass immigration of Russian Jews to Israel and the United States in recent years.

---

130 Remnick, „Native Son,“ *New York Review of Books*, 14 February 1991, 10.
131 Solzhenitsyn, *Dvesti let vmeste*, 7.

Despite the bewilderment *Two Hundred Years Together* is galvanizing, the mere fact that Solzhenitsyn considers the modern Russo-Jewish Question a worthy subject for research should encourage his readership to reassess this history, if only out of respect for the author. For Solzhenitsyn's opponents, however, this is not the issue at hand. Few would dispute the writer's literary gift and the linguistic vitality with which he could compose such a work; objections are heard among Jews who would not have their nation's role in Russian history assessed by a purported anti-Semite. It seems no matter what Solzhenitsyn states or writes, he cannot absolve himself of this racial stigma. The author further explains his literary intention:

> My book aims to go deep into Jewish thoughts, feelings, ideas, and mentality—that is to say, the realm of the spiritual. In this sense the objective of my book is not, in fact, scientific, but artistic. It is basically an artistic work. Except that there are not two or three characters, but a great many characters, with various, most diverse feelings and ideas. Facts alone are not enough to understand them. Generally speaking, I regard the spirit and conscience as the most substantial elements of history.[132]

The author fully appreciates the "metaphysical" facets of the Jewish Question. He even suggests that such a question may prove to be comprehensible in only religious and mystical planes.

Appealing to both sides, both Jewish and Russian, Solzhenitsyn admonishes all to come and submissively share in the blame of Russia's past. The author has conveyed a desire to avoid this "thorny thicket" of history and actually earlier hoped that another writer would undertake to generously and equitably illuminate the Russo-Jewish Question:

> Я не терял надежды, что найдётся прежде меня автор, кто объёмно и равновесно, обоесторонне осветит нам этот калёный клин. Но чаще встречаем укоры односторонние: либо о вине русских перед евреями, даже об извечной испорченности русского народа, — это-

132 Victor Loshak, „Russians? Jews? Russian Jews?," http://english.mn.ru/english/issue.php?2002-51-9.

> го с избытком. Либо, с другой стороны: кто из русских об этой взаимной проблеме писал — то большей частью запальчиво, переклонно, не желая и видеть, что бы зачесть другой стороне в заслугу.[133]

Unsatisfied with the scholarship devoted to this history, Solzhenitsyn's fear of his own eventual end bade him take up the pen.[134]

Aleksandr Isaeivich undoubtedly had been considering the idea for a treatise such as *Two Hundred Years Together* as early as the alleged essay from the 1960s. Later, as a political exile in Vermont, the writer repeatedly encountered the Jewish Question whilst involved in *The Red Wheel.* In spite of this, he did not feel it prudent to address the incendiary topic with incomplete research, nor did he intend for *The Red Wheel* to take such a controversial slant. The series was to be dedicated to the Russian Revolution. The Jewish Question, as he would later discover, could have bled disproportionately into *The Red Wheel,* creating an unbalanced emphasis. The theme, nonetheless, remained historically relevant and yet under-researched in his eyes. Consequently, it became the fruit of a nearly ten-year labor. In spite of his critics, Solzhenitsyn pronounced such a literary work culturally essential for the healing and normalization of Russo-Jewish social thought.

For quite some time Russo-Jewish history (especially of the Soviet era) has had a forbidden feel attached to it in the Russian press, not to mention a perception that the best thing a Russian could do for his fellow Jewish comrades is to not bring up Jewish issues at all. The author insists that the Jewish Question cannot remain a taboo subject for thoughtful students of Russian history and for historians of the modern world. That said, he feels it is crucial for historians to assess with discretion the dynamic story of these two great ethnic groups, displaying scrupulous respect for fact and being sensitive to volatile national passions. Solzhenitsyn expresses disapproval of extremist elements on the Russian political right which recklessly blame Jews for the 70-year Communist malady, whilst he simultaneously condemns the inordinate number of Jews who, he feels, should express contrition for their role in revolutionary movements. In essence, he seeks to walk the "middle line" and

133 Aleksandr Solzhenitsyn, „Dvesti let vmeste," http://sila.by.ru/.
134 Solzhenitsyn, *Dvesti let vmeste*, 5.

is duly criticized for it. Referring to Solzhenitsyn's criticism of Jews who took privileged jobs as trustees in the camps, Semyon Reznik writes: "Однако не всех зэков-евреев Солженицын гребет под *придурочную* гребенку! Он признает, что бывали и исключения, то есть бывали в лагерях и хорошие евреи. Без них никак нельзя: не выдержать средней линнии."[135] Any grace Solzhenitsyn shows to a Jew is seen as disingenuous adherence to the golden mean. The writer, however, has long seen the wisdom of the "middle point of view" as he expressed in *October 1916*:

> По еврейскому вопросу все спешат занять только одну из самых крайных позиций. Или евреи—это невинно страдающая масса благородных характеров, которых надо как одно целое непременно любить, и даже отдельных недоступно порицать, ибо упрёк разложится на всех. Или это—сплошь тёмные злобные заговорщики, которых как единое целое можно только ненавидеть, и подозрительно, когда любят хоть отдельных из них. И всякая попытка ввести оговорку, не сплошь нежно любить или не сплошь страстно ненавидеть, отталкивается с негодованием каждой из сторон. *Но в тысячах вопросов бывает плодотворна лишь средняя точка зрения.*[136]

Does the Jewish Question truly wash over the face of modern Russia, demanding a behemoth work such as *Two Hundred Years Together*? This query would undoubtedly receive a mixed response. As the work approached publication Solzhenitsyn sensed not only immediate umbrage from Jews and non-Jews alike for engaging in a work dedicated solely to the Jewish Question, but also a "ring of resentment" and brazen refusal to read his book.[137] Furthermore, certain important Jewish political figures and historians questioned the author's intention in writing it, attributing a subconscious need to fan the flames of anti-Semitism in Russia. "Solzhenitsyn's book is anti-Semitic and mendacious," claimed Victor Dashevsky of the Moscow anti-Fascist Cen-

---

135 Semyon Reznik, *Vmeste ili vroz': Zametki na poliakh A.I. Solzhenitsyna* (Moskva: Zakharov, 2003), 417.

136 Aleksandr Solzhenitsyn, *Oktiabr' 1916* (Paris: YMCA Press, 1984), 45 [emphasis added-NL].

137 Loshak, „Russians? Jews? Russian Jews?".

tre.[138] In contrast, others, including Jews, have expressed gratitude for the writer's desire to heal past wounds and achieve Russo-Jewish mutual understanding. "Solzhenitsyn is not an anti-Semite. He remains a banner of my generation, for Jews and non-Jews," remarked Mark Kajdan, a Jewish researcher with the Russian Academy of Sciences.[139] Moreover, Shimon Peres, Israeli Foreign Minister of Belorussian origin, expressed "pleasant surprise" at having learned Solzhenitsyn was involved in a book addressing relations between Jews and Russians.[140] Clearly there is an unmistakable disparity in opinion of Aleksandr Isaievich among Russian Jewish intellectuals.

A Brief Exegesis of *Two Hundred Years Together, part II*

Two Hundred Years Together is somewhat of a departure from the Nobel Laureate's past works. Although much of the writer's catalogue reflects his personal interpretation of history (and despite his claim that his project is "literary"), this latest offering is not a work of fiction but an academic/artistic piece of writing. The pages are adorned with profuse citations, while sources range from Soviet archives, to memoirs by Jews, and to pages of the Israeli press. Undoubtedly Solzhenitsyn intended to present a highly transparent, objective text. A more curious aspect of *Two Hundred Years Together* is that it does not flow as a traditional historical account, but more like a conversation—driven not by events, but ideas. These ideas are distilled into a virtual catechism put to the reader, posing seemingly rhetorical questions—although at times Solzhenitsyn is guilty of providing his own answers.

In his desire to minimize personal Russian bias, Solzhenitsyn begins part II of *Two Hundred Years Together* by discrediting the common post-Soviet nationalist contention that Bolshevism was born entirely of Jewish impetus. He further demonstrates that the 1917 Revolutions of both February and October were predominantly the work of Russian hands, but he empha-

---

138 „Russian Jews charge Solzhenitsyn with altering history," http://www.jewishsf.com/content/2-0-/module/displaystory/story_id/16730/format/html/displaystory.html.

139 Ibid.

140 Marcus Warren, „Solzhenitsyn tries to heal Jewish wounds:[Daily Edition]," http://pqasb.pqarchiver.com/jpost/.

sizes his belief that Jews stood to gain the most from the dissolution of the monarchy—receiving access to higher education, professional guilds, and politics, as well as rights to live in Moscow and Petrograd. Solzhenitsyn acknowledges that for Russian Jews there was really very little to be desired in the continuation of the *ancien régime*. Indeed, the socialist future seemed to present great opportunity and long-awaited egalitarianism. Thus in a way he exonerates Jews for their participation, at least in the February revolution, stating that it was understandable considering Jewish social circumstances. In his chapter on the February Revolution he writes:

> По многолетней и подробностной моей работе мне досталось осмыслять суть Февральской революции, заодно и еврейскую в ней роль. Я вывел для себя и могу теперь повторить: нет, Февральскую революцию — не евреи сделали русским, она была совершена, несомненно, самими русскими, — и, я думаю, я достаточно это показал в «Красном Колесе». Мы сами совершили это крушение: наш миропомазанный царь, придворные круги, высшие бесталанные генералы, задубевшие администраторы, с ними заодно их противники — избранная интеллигенция, октябристы, земцы, кадеты, революционные демократы, социалисты и революционеры, — и с ними же заодно разбойная часть запасников, издевательски содержимых в петербургских казармах. И именно в этом шла к нам гибель. Среди-то интеллигенции уже было много евреев — но это никак не даёт основания назвать революцию еврейской.[141]

Solzhenitsyn's more avid critics have focused their discontent upon the direction the work takes following these attempts to understand the Jewish dilemma during the Revolution. For nearly two chapters, Jews who were pivotal in the rise of Bolshevism are listed by name and background history. This cumbersome information might be thought his most uninviting prose to date. He conveys the impression that Jews provided the brains as well as the rank and file of the Communist movement thereafter, whilst simultaneously acknowledging that this did not mean a dearth of revolutionaries among the

---

141 Solzhenitsyn, *Dvesti let vmeste*, 41.

Russians. Special attention is allotted to Leon Trotsky, leader of the Red Army during the Civil War, whom the writer feels epitomizes the rootless internationalist aspiration of many Diaspora Jews. Page after page he examines this early volatile history, with great contempt expressed for Russians who committed atrocities against Jews. In these moments the writer's national bias is quite apparent: although aware of the anti-Jewish pogroms and condemning them, he rhetorically queries whether anything else could have been expected given the perceived association between Jews and Bolshevism in the mind of the masses.

Although it is thought by some Jews only to incite anti-Semitism, much research has been done on Jewish participation in the revolutionary movement (some of which Solzhenitsyn includes in his own account). Richard Pipes states: "The number of Jews active in Communism in Russia and abroad was striking: in Hungary, for example they furnished 90 percent of the leading figures in Bela Kun's dictatorship. They were disproportionately represented among Communists in Germany and Austria during the revolutionary upheavals there in 1918–23, and in the apparatus of the Communist International."[142] According to other accounts, by the time the Bolshevik regime was firmly in place in Russia there were high numbers of Jews among members of the new one-party state. W. E. Mosse asserts that although Jews comprised less than 4% of the population, approximately 17–25% of the prominent Russian revolutionaries in the early 1920s were of Jewish extraction.[143] Another provocative viewpoint was put forth by Dr. Wladimir Krysko who observed: "It was not a matter of great note that the Jews were playing a large role in the remaking of Russia, because Jews represented the only group of people destined by their own history to lead a New Order which was going to . . . promote international brotherhood."[144] In this vein D. M. Thomas remarked: "Intelligent and dynamic, Jews played a predominant part in the Bolshevik revolution as they played in the creation of psychoanalysis, modern physics, and modernism in art."[145] Some Jews accept such interpretations, others vehemently refute them as anti-Semitic rhetoric, and yet others believe

142 Richard Pipes, *Russia under the Bolshevik Regime* (New York: Alfred A. Knopf, 1994), 112.

143 W. E. Mosse, „Makers of the Soviet Union," *Slavonic Review* 46 (1968), 148.

144 Wladimir W. Krysko, *I Choose the Truth* (unpublished memoir), 48.

145 Thomas, *Aleksandr Solzhenitsyn: A Century in His Life*, 493.

it is not yet the right time to discuss such incendiary issues at all. One of Solzhenitsyn's critics, Andrei Siniavsky, questions the writer's judgment in ascribing pivotal influence to the Jews:

> How could a handful of strangers subjugate a country as huge as Russia? It was all far more complicated than Solzhenitsyn would have it. As for the notion that the Jews fomented revolutionary trouble, it was first spread at the turn of the century by the tsarist secret police—by the Black Hundred. As a matter of fact, the Jews who became revolutionaries gave up their Jewish identity completely to serve the revolution. The idea of a Jewish plot against the integrity of Russia is absurd, an old myth of the far right.[146]

Thus by no means are all ethnic Russian intellectuals content with the thrust of Solzhenitsyn's exposition; although, as we have seen, he explicitly rejects the notion that Russia and Russians were the victims of a Jewish revolution.

Solzhenitsyn's account assumes a new vivacity when crossing the threshold into his own lifetime. Although he is able to speak from first-hand experience in the camps and prisons, he steps into dangerous territory with his outspoken account of Jews in the Gulag. For example, he writes in *Two Hundred Years Together* Part II: "И если я захотел бы *обобщить,* что евреям в лагерях жилось особенно тяжело, — мне это будет разрешено, и я не буду осыпан упрёками за несправедливое национальное обобщение. Но в лагерях, где я сидел, было иначе: *евреям, насколько обобщать можно, жилось легче, чем остальным.*"[147] According to Solzhenitsyn's observations, Jews serving as commandants saw to it that other Jews were not subjected to the standard evils of camp life—Jewish doctors exempted their own from hard labor, psychiatric wards (which were said to be the most comfortable parts of camp) were replete with Jews, and Jews made up a clear preponderance in the Gulag administration. Many Jews dispute

---

146 Andrei Sinyavsky and Olga Andreyev Carlisle, „Solzhenitsyn and Russian Nationalism: An Interview with Andrei Siniavsky," http://www.nybooks.com/articles/article-preview?article_id=7611.

147 Solzhenitsyn, *Dvesti let vmeste*, 331 [latter emphasis added-NL].

these claims and are affronted by what they see as the author's inaccurate and unjust assessment of the Gulag history. Again, it is perhaps Solzhenitsyn's relentless candor and brutal honesty that, whether right or wrong, earn him the name anti-Semite: he cites all of these examples of nepotism as Jewish vengeance for the sins against their race in Russia's monarchical past.

Moving along into the book's account of the Second World War, Solzhenitsyn provides a meticulous history of the Nazi Holocaust within the Soviet Union and condemns the inertia on the part of all to help Jews who fell into the clutches of Hitler's ethnic annihilation. As to Jewish loyalty, the author refutes the notion that Jews were underrepresented in the Red Army defense of Soviet lands. In no other army, not even the American army, did Jews occupy such high ranks as in that of the Soviet Union, believes Solzhenitsyn, saying this was by virtue of the numerous Russian Jews with higher education. Given this, he reminds the reader satirically that many Jews stayed away from the front due to "divided loyalties" (двойное подданство): a politico-cultural dilemma that some Diaspora Jews have encountered when compelled to take up arms. Although Hitler's plan of Jewish genocide was slow to disseminate within the Soviet press, many Jews joined the ranks with great enthusiasm once news of the Holocaust had reached them.

What many find troubling, Jews and non-Jews alike, is the Old Testament prophet-like manner of Solzhenitsyn's categorical interpretations of Judeo-Russian history: he is accused of assuming a tone presaging divine retribution for both Jewish and Russian sins committed as collective nationalities. Among the profuse citations and carefully posed rhetorical questions, such "prophetic" unequivocal statements are few, yet relatively salient. He concludes chapter 21 on the Jewish role in World War II thus:

> До такой достойной, великодушной самокритичности — подниматься бы и русским умам в суждениях о российской истории XX века — от озверения революционного периода, через запуганное равнодушие советского, и до грабительской мерзости послесоветского. В невыносимой тяжести сознания, что в этом веке мы, русские, обрушили свою историю — через негодных правителей, но и

> через собственную негодность, — из гложущей тревоге, что это, может быть, непоправимо, — увидеть и в русском опыте: не наказание ли то от *Высшей Силы*?[148]

He is careful though. When directed towards Jews, such ideas speaking of "divine retribution" are often first expressed through the voice of a Jew with similar beliefs. Whether or not he does this to show overwhelming evidence for his views, or as in Andrei Rogachevsky's words, "to hide behind the scholarship of others,"[149] is difficult to deduce. For example, historian Daniel Levin's words accompany Solzhenitsyn as the latter delves into explanations of the "catastrophic" Holocaust as a punishment for Jewish spiritual apostasy, turning away from the Torah, and embracing Bolshevism. Levin is quoted in *Two Hundred Years Together* saying: "Катастрофа была в значительной мере наказанием за грехи, в том числе—за грех руководства коммунистическим движением. В этом что-то есть."[150] Solzhenitsyn's excerpt above speaks primarily of Russian guilt before a "Higher Power" and thus makes a plea to collectively share the guilt for the plague of Communism.

Did the Jews have a choice? This question is likewise implied in *Two Hundred Years Together* and rears its head as one digs deeper into Russo-Jewish Soviet history. It is the early history of the Soviet regime and the attributes of its pivotal figures which are important because they foreshadowed the Soviet treachery that overran Russia and Eastern Europe. Although such generalizations do not define every Jew who was deceived by Soviet ideology, the response of the Jewish community as a whole is distressing to many, including Solzhenitsyn. Most importantly, it is the crux of the Jewish Question in Soviet-Russian history.

The years of World War II offer unique insight. From a certain perspective the Jewish community in Russia (and even those who fled eastward into Russia) faced a terrible dilemma: a choice had to be made between the lesser of two evils—Soviet Communism or German Fascism. Acquiescence in the former was certainly not without peril, but it did offer a chance of sur-

---

148 Ibid., 390 [emphasis added-NL].

149 Andrei Rogachevskii, „Review of Aleksandr Solzhenitsyn, Dvesti let vmeste (1795–1995), Part II (Moscow, 2002)," *East European Jewish Affairs* 33 (2003), 130.

150 Daniel Levin, „Na kraiu soblaznu:[interview]," *22*, no.1 (1978), 55.

vival. The latter choice, however, ultimately meant an unquestionable violent end. However, this we know only with hindsight, whereas Jews who had had only two decades to understand the measure of Soviet power would have had little awareness of the Holocaust. The unfortunate fact which is outlined in the second volume of *Two Hundred Years Together* is that scores of Jews did not simply subordinate themselves to Soviet ideology in some sentiment of neutrality. Many embraced it whole-heartedly. Like those of their own who in the days of the Revolution fell victim to the "Communist lie," rising to administrative ranks, and later taking part in the Great Terror, many not only found refuge in Bolshevism but embraced it and further contributed to its cruelty. Was there more to the Jewish espousal of Bolshevism than its idealization by comparison with Hitler's bane? In due course, Solzhenitsyn writes not only of the perilous repercussions of Jewish involvement in the Soviet experiment, but also the impiety of contributing to atrocity in a country in which one is an ethnic minority. For Solzhenitsyn, the espousal of evil is never the only way out. One always has a choice. He writes:

> Не было *выхода*? А тем десяткам тысяч российских чиновников, отказавшихся служить большевизму, — разве было куда податься? Умереть с голоду? — а на что жили горожане не-евреи? Да ещё была ведь помощь Джойнта, ОРТа и подобное снабжение от щедрых евреев с Запада? Идти на службу в ЧК — это никогда не *единственный* выход. Есть по крайней мере ещё один — не идти, выстаивать.[151]

The central themes of Solzhenitsyn's *Two Hundred Years Together* have been investigated by others including Latvian scholar George Irbe, who classifies this social phenomenon as the "new" Jewish Question. Its basis addresses Jewish involvement in atrocities befalling Russia during and after the October Revolution, especially in the Red Terror poured out upon Russia and Eastern European nations which, following the Hitler-Stalin Pact of 1939, fell under Soviet hegemony. The post-Soviet context of a "new" Jewish Question is not the dreadful Nazi *Judenfrage*, nor even the "Jewish Question" proposed

151 Solzhenitsyn, *Dvesti let vmeste*, 101.

by Karl Marx. A "new" Jewish Question emerging since the fall of the Soviet regime seems to be taking shape, the premise of which some Jewish scholars (including names such as Israel Shamir) believe the Jewish race partially brings upon itself. Although only an extreme minority denies the evil nature of atrocities inflicted upon Jews during the twentieth century and the Holocaust in particular, scholars and writers espousing opinions similar to those of Solzhenitsyn suggest that at times Jews aggravate age-old anti-Semitism by denying national complicity in the Red Terror (a Holocaust which by some measures may have been more costly and longer-lasting than Hitler's). Certain Jewish scholars, such as Noam Chomsky, while wanting the world to forever remember the attempted extermination of Jews under Nazi Germany, object to the unabashed exploitation of a "Holocaust industry" by opportunists and the insensitive manner in which many Holocaust-boosters downplay or even fail to acknowledge the suffering of millions under the Red Terror. Scores of members of the Nazi party, whether dead or living, have been identified as responsible for their respective crimes against humanity and tried accordingly. What is more, many German citizens even from the post-World War II generation have expressed a sentiment of continued national repentance for the blood spilt by their countrymen half a century ago. In spite of this, as Solzhenitsyn points out, many Jews remain in relative denial of collective guilt wrought by their own in the Soviet Union during the Red Terror. *The Black Book of Communism* reads:

> Scholars have neglected the crimes committed by the Communists. While names such as Himmler and Eichmann are recognized around the world as bywords for twentieth century barbarism, the names such as Feliks Dzerzhinsky, Genrikh Iagoda, and Nikolai Ezhov languish in obscurity. . . . The revelations concerning Communist crimes cause barely a stir . . . there is widespread reluctance to make such a crucial factor as a crime—mass crime, systematic crime, and crime against humanity—a central factor in the analysis of Communism.[152]

---

[152] Stéphane Courtois et al., *The Black Book of Communism: Crimes, Terror, Repression*, trans. Jonathan Murphy (London: Harvard University Press, 1999), 17.

Two Hundred Years Together presents a series of complex questions: Can a nation or people be judged as a collective whole? Does an individual Russian or Jew answer in some sense for the sins of the nation from whence he sprang? How are Jews of the rising generation to relate to this page of history? Throughout volume two of *Two Hundred Years Together* Solzhenitsyn addresses such queries. Just as nations must exhibit collective repentance in order to bring social healing, so nations, he believes, can be judged as a whole as long as such judgment is equitable and made with a genuine understanding of human imperfection. Clear distinctions are drawn between different Jewish social strata, and he cites the case of Jews who rushed headlong into the revolution, of others who provided the labor for the mammoth Soviet military-industrial complex, and of those who abstained altogether. "Jews and Russians," he argues, "worked together to oppress Jews, Russians, and a myriad other nations. Russians have recognized their guilt; it is time for Jews to do the same, and just as Russians are wrong to blame Jews for all of their ills, so are Jews wrong to scapegoat Russians."[153]

But is Solzhenitsyn just in demanding collective Jewish contrition for Bolshevik atrocities? Were leading Jewish Communists such as Trotsky living in accordance with Judaic traditions? It is arguable that those Jews who played pioneering roles in the October Revolution and subsequent Red Terror were not Jews in spirit, but apostates. For that matter, Russians subscribing to the Soviet "end justifies the means" rhetoric that cost the lives of millions were no more "Russian" in spirit either. One can interpret such individuals of any race as traitors to their own nation. Solzhenitsyn believes that Bolshevik leaders were rootless traitors of Russian, Jewish, Georgian, and Polish ethnicities. All ethnic roots had been severed with the adoption of Marxism-Leninism and what resulted was an ambiguous international cultural *mélange* without nationhood. However, the high numbers of Jews among the revolutionaries demonstrates that Jews who jettison their religion and turn their backs on their people become uprooted and hence capable of the wildest excesses. Although somewhat counter-intuitive, perhaps this does not detract from Judaism, but redounds, on the contrary, to its praise.

153 Lydia Chukovskaya, „Interview with Solzhenitsyn about 'Two Hundred Years Together,'" http://www.orthodoxytoday.org/articles/ChukovskayaSolzhenitsyn.htm.

Solzhenitsyn is aware of the questions raised and addresses them in *Two Hundred Years Together* via his own rhetorical questions: How much evidence must there be of the participation of traitors before one can acknowledge a pattern that defies random distribution? What fraction of the Jewish nation is required to be involved? How widely and actively did Jews participate in strengthening Bolshevik authority? And again: What was the reaction of nationals of each group's people to the traitors from its ranks? The reactions of people to traitors can vary—they can curse them or praise them, ostracize them or join them. The manifestations of this—the reactions of the masses of the people, whether Russian or Jewish—have been given very little consideration by historians. Solzhenitsyn believes the Russian traitors are known and the depressing number that joined the Bolsheviks is unpardonable.

Part of the rhetoric surrounding the Jewish Question at the advent of Communism was the previously mentioned idea of a "non-national" character, particularly as expressed in the writings of Vladimir Lenin and Lev Trotsky. The latter, born in a Jewish family of Ukraine, stated "I am not a Jew, but an internationalist." Trotsky's international, cosmopolitan worldview was not uncommon among Jewish communities, especially when discontent loomed within a given host nation. In *Two Hundred Years Together* Solzhenitsyn suggests this dearth of national awareness was the explicit rationale in Leninist Bolshevism and often was a factor as Russian Jews jumped aboard the Communist bandwagon. Jews possessed neither a common territory nor a common language; although many spoke Yiddish, many did not. Even Lenin, with all of his internationalist aspiration, found it difficult to classify the Jews. The best he could do was to define them as a "special oppressed caste." He further stated: "The great world-progressive features of Jewish culture have clearly made themselves felt: its internationalism, its responsiveness to the advanced movements of the epoch (the percentage of Jews in the democratic and proletarian movement is everywhere higher than the percentage of Jews in the population as a whole)."[154]

---

154 Vladimir Lenin, „Critical Remarks on the National Question," http://www.marx2mao.org/Lenin/CRNQ13.htm.

Repentance

In the search for mutual reconciliation between the two nationalities, the theme of repentance takes on a central role throughout *Two Hundred Years Together*, is aired both implicitly and explicitly, and addresses Russians and Jews alike. Since Solzhenitsyn claims that Jewish participation in the revolution far exceeded their proportionate numbers in the Russian population, an acknowledgement of that complicity should be made by Jews collectively as a nation or ethnic group. In an interview with Viktor Loshak on the publication of the new book, the topic of repentance is mentioned:

> *Loshak*: 'Am I right to understand that in the first chapters of Book 2, devoted to the Revolution, you disclose the Russian *noms de guerre* of Jewish revolutionaries and count their number in the supreme Revolutionary bodies so as to show in the closing chapters, when talking about the need for nationwide repentance, that Jews have cause not only to resent Soviet power, but also to repent?'
>
> *Solzhenitsyn*: 'That's right, both.'[155]

To conceptualize Solzhenitsyn's point on "collective repentance," it is worth recalling first that he sets the highest value on the existence of the nation which, in his words of 1973, constitutes "a complex, vivid, unrepeatable organism not invented by man."[156] The idea of "national repentance" is alien in some respects even to Western philosophies of nationhood, but Solzhenitsyn firmly believes it is a necessary part of social healing. He is convinced of the naturalness and need for "transferability" of ethical judgments from the individual to social strata and ultimately to the political sphere. Nations, he believes, are "vital formations" that, similar to their individual parts, can experience pangs of conscience and the painful step of mutual contrition. Dostoevsky's *Diary of a Writer* is cited, which speaks of the indebtedness of every nation to a prior spiritual idea as well as the "right" of a people to preserve its national soul through repentance. Because life is so fleeting, a nation can no

155 Chukovskaia, „Interview with Solzhenitsyn."
156 Solzhenitsyn, *From Under the Rubble*, 110.

more survive spiritually than can an individual under the weight of sin. In Solzhenitsyn's mind, a new generation does not begin anew, so to speak; Chesterton's famous "democracy of the dead" unites a nation in a community of guilt and remorse.

As Solzhenitsyn states in the interview cited above, he encourages national repentance for both Jews and Russians. Hence when he speaks of Jewish contrition for Bolshevik crimes it should be noted that this reflects an all-inclusive call to social compunction. Many of the writer's efforts to address social ills upon his return home in 1994 show that, first and foremost, he advocates repentance on the part of his own nationality. He insists that Russians, Belorussians, and Ukrainians share the principal burden of Communist malefaction and every Russian bears some level of responsibility for Communism. In his view very few eluded its scourge, nearly all adapted to living by the ideocratic lie. In his essay "Repentance and Self Limitation in the Life of Nations," he speaks of unambiguous Russian blameworthiness for the past:

> This realm of darkness, of falsehood, of brute force, of justice denied and distrust of the good, this slimy swamp was formed by *us*, and no one else. We grew used to the idea that we must submit and lie in order to survive—and we brought up our children to do so. Each of us, if he honestly reviews the life he has led, without special pleading or concealment, will recall more than one occasion in which he pretended not to hear a cry for help, averted his indifferent eyes from an imploring gaze, burned letters and photographs which it was his duty to keep, forgot someone's name or dropped certain windows, turned his back on prisoners under escort, and—but of course—always voted, rose to his feet and applauded obscenities . . . how, otherwise, could he survive? How, moreover, could the great Archipelago have endured in our midst for fifty years unnoticed?[157]

This penitent evaluation of Russia reflects the writer's advocacy of his nation's need for repentance. Words such as *us* denote not simply individuals

---

157 Ibid., 118.

falling victim to the lie but his nation as a whole. Within this vein consider also a very recent prose poem by Aleksandr Solzhenitsyn. It is one of a series recently published in English translation in the appendix of Joseph Pearce's 1999 biography, *Solzhenitsyn: A Soul in Exile*. The poem, translated by Michael Nicholson and Alexis Klimoff, is entitled "Shame":

> How agonizing is it to feel shame for your own Motherland?
>
> Whose callous hands are these, whose scheming hands that rule Her life so rashly and corruptly? What faces these—haughty, cunning or void of character—that represent Her to the world? What rancid swill is She in place of wholesome spiritual fare? To what depths of ruin and penury are Her people reduced, powerless to clamber from the pit?
>
> The sense of humiliation is unremitting. It has none of the transience of those everyday personal emotions, which change readily to match the fleeting play of circumstance. No, it oppresses you constantly, dogs your every step—it is with you when you wake, with you as you drag out each hour of the day and with you as you sink back into night. And even in death, which sets us free from personal afflictions, can offer no escape from this Shame—it will simply continue to hang over the heads of the living, and you, after all, are a particle of their being.
>
> You peruse the depths of Russia's past in search of encouraging precedents. And yet you know equally well the implacable truth—that nations of the earth have sometimes perished utterly. This would not be the first time.
>
> But no, there are other depths to draw upon—those two dozen regions of the Russian heartland that I visited on my travels—it is they that whisper words of hope to me. There I saw aspirations still untarnished, a questing spirit as yet uncrushed, and living, generous-hearted countrymen of mine. Can it be that they will never break out of this pale of doom? No—they shall break free! It is yet within their power.

> But day after day the Shame hangs over us, like a pinkish-yellow cloud of poisonous gas, corroding our lungs. And even when at last it is dispersed, the blot upon history will never be erased.[158]

The feeling of shame is what an individual or a body politic undergoes as a preface to repentance. When assessing Solzhenitsyn's calls for repentance on the part of Russian Jews it is important to remember that he both feels contrition for his own Communist past and demands it from his countrymen.

Assimilation

The conclusion of *Two Hundred Years Together* examines Jewish assimilation. The author alludes to the difficulties of ethnic assimilation in the following words:

> Русский еврей... Еврей, русский... Сколько вокруг этого соединения-разделения ролилось крови, слёз, сколько нагромоздилось несказанных страданий, которым ещё не видать конца, и сколько здесь всё же было радости духовного и культурного роста... Было и осталось очень много евреев, которые подняли на свои плечи этот тяжкий крест: быть русским евреем и русским. Две любви, две страсти, два борения... Не слишком ли много для одного сердца? Да, слишком много. Но в этом и состоит фатальный трагизм этого двуединства. От слова не станется, и двуединство — всё-таки не есть единство. Здесь равновесие — не данность, а заданность.[159]

By the late Soviet era and even into the post-Soviet period, most Russian Jews remaining in Russia had been assimilated to some degree or another. Many in this group possess a self-identity embracing both ethnic Russianness and Jewishness. Yet a suspicious attitude toward Jewish assimi-

---

158 Aleksandr Solzhenitsyn, „Shame," in Joseph Pearce, *Solzhenitsyn: A Soul in Exile* (Grand Rapids: Baker Books, 1999), 324–325.

159 S. Ivanovich, *Semyon Yushkevich i evrei*, (Ierusalim: E. Kapitaikina, 1992), 29.

lated identity is rife, especially among Russian nationalists. Solzhenitsyn, no doubt because of his deeply spiritual beliefs of nationhood, has often had difficulty accepting that Jews can really be considered Russian. Nevertheless, in an ambiguous way, assimilation is held up as his preferred solution. The word "assimilation" is used repeatedly, though without recognition of the contentious undertone of the term, or the enormous literature on the subject. In Solzhenitsyn's account, "assimilation" is something which the Russian government offered to the Jews and which they repeatedly rejected. When he does recognize episodes of successful assimilation, he laments that it is in vain: Jews assimilated, but not with the people—with the minority group of self-alienated Russian intelligentsia. As a result, assimilated Jews became revolutionaries or liberals, proliferating the destructive influence of both on the Russian state.

As for the Jewish Question as a whole, Solzhenitsyn appears unresolved about Jewish assimilation within the Russian state. "So far, assimilation has not been very convincing," he writes. "The problem of assimilation remains difficult to resolve. And although from a broad perspective the process of assimilation has gone quite far, we cannot then conclude that the Diaspora has been dismantled."[160] Although he desires the coexistence of the two nations, it likely requires too great a cultural-religious sacrifice. Jews who are successful in assimilation are, by most accounts, those who relinquish their religious legacy in order to adopt the culture and nationhood of their host country. The idea of renouncing one's faith would be in Solzhenitsyn's eyes ethically and spiritually unacceptable, regardless of the religion in question. The issue becomes more complex when considering the many Jewish Bolsheviks who were ostensibly "assimilated" Jews and had genuinely given up their religion, but for what he would deem malign purposes. Hence the problem with assimilation. For this reason the writer has for many years now encouraged Jewish emigration to Israel.

160 Sam Greene, „Solzhenitsyn and the Jews," http://mailman.lbo-talk.org/2003/2003-March/007454.html.

XI *The Protocols of the Elders of Zion*

Discussion of Judeo-Russian history invariably recalls the mysterious document *The Protocols of the Elders of Zion*. Since the publication of *Jews in the USSR and in Future Russia* and *Two Hundred Years Together*, Solzhenitsyn's name has come up in connection with the *Protocols*. Many scholars consider the writings a forgery, while others suggest they should be thought of as "pseudo-epigrapha," a political pamphlet of sorts, albeit with uncertain origins. To be sure, attributing authenticity to the *Protocols* has proven knotty over the last century; in many ways the document has acquired the character of a palimpsest and most scholars simply steer clear of the question "Who wrote them?" Through the years the *Protocols* have gained status as a potent intellectual weapon of anti-Semitism, drawn on by despots such as Adolph Hitler, who writes in *Mein Kampf*: *"Wie sehr das ganze Dasein dieses Volkes auf einer fortlaufenden Lüge beruht, wird in unvergleichlicher Art in den von den Juden so unendlich gehaßten Protokollen der Weisen von Zion gezeigt."*[161] Despite the tragedy of the Holocaust and the indications that the work is indeed a forgery, copies of the *Protocols* are still being printed and disseminated even today.

The Protocols of the Elders of Zion is likely the most widespread and successful written work of modern-day anti-Semitism. Although quite sensational and couched in a tone of conspiracy theory in the purest sense, this document has been analyzed and cited for over two centuries. It came into the spotlight in the United States under the auspices of Henry Ford, and although Winston Churchill did not explicitly endorse the *Protocols*, he wrote in their rhetorical tone, speaking of a "worldwide Jewish overthrow of civilization" in a Sunday Herald article on 8 February 1920. In the twenty-first century, anti-Semitism emanating from the *Protocols* is still on the rise as racism against Jews escalates in Europe and especially in the Middle East. With this in mind, any objective analysis of *The Protocols of the Elders of Zion*—which

161 Adolf Hitler, *Mein Kampf* (Boston: Houghton Mifflin, 2001), 337.

appears to have been Solzhenitsyn's aim—is likely to be viewed with suspicion by critics.

The *Protocols*' origins draw on the enduring anti-Semitism derived from medieval Europe at the time of the Crusades. The belief that Jews used blood from Christian infants for rituals and poisoned wells in order to spread the Bubonic Plague provided pretexts for the horrific destruction of Jewish communities in Europe. During this era, stories were disseminated of secret Jewish cabals whose alleged purpose it was to subjugate and annihilate Christians. The *Protocols* appear to have had their origin shortly after the time of the French Revolution. In 1806 a French Jesuit by the name of Abbe Barruel sent out what was presumed to be a forged letter by the state police opposed to Napoleon Bonaparte's liberal stance concerning the Jews. The document accused Jews of a conspiracy that had earlier been attributed to Freemasons, and eventually the work turned up in Poland and Germany later in the nineteenth century. Scholars have found that the direct predecessor of the *Protocols* originates in a pamphlet entitled *Dialogues in Hell Between Machiavelli and Montesquieu*, which was published in 1864 by a French satirist called Maurice Joly. The document actually makes no mention of Jews, but of Emperor Napoleon III's political ambitions. These dialogues subsequently fell into the hands of German anti-Semite Herman Goedsche who worked as a spy for the Prussian Secret Police. Goedsche allegedly adapted Joly's dialogues into a story of Jewish conspiracy as a part of a novel series called "Biarritz" appearing in 1868.

The *Protocols* eventually appeared in Russia having been translated in 1872. There is little doubt that these writings provided the Russian Secret Police with a convenient pretext for discrediting Tsar Nicholas II's reforms, which had softened the plight of the Jews in the empire. The manuscripts were edited into their final form in 1895 and were published in Russian two years later. They did not, however, become publicly known until 1905, at which time Russia was suffering humiliating defeat in the Russo-Japanese War and boiling over in early revolutionary activity. These dynamic events were followed by the promulgation of a new constitution and the institution of a short-lived *Duma*. As a result, the intransigent *Union of the Russian Nation* or *Black Hundred* organization provoked popular discontent with Russian Jews who were scapegoated for an "un-Russian" constitution and the bloody 1905

Revolution. For this purpose the *Protocols* were published in a public journal by Sergius Nilus in 1905 as part of a propaganda scheme accompanying pogroms incited by the Russian Secret Police. In the following two years, modified texts of the *Protocols* were published by George Bumti which found their way into the possession of the Tsar. Although Nicholas II is said to have believed the *Protocols* a forgery, they nonetheless remained in his keep and were used by the Whites during the Civil War to catalyze widespread persecution against Jews, believed to be well represented in the Red Army.

In these very same years the *Protocols* were brought into Western Europe by Russian emigrants whereupon the Nilus edition was translated into several languages. In 1920 they appeared in London and were immediately declared a forgery by Lucien Wolf who exposed the forged work of Joly and Goedsche in a publication of the Jewish Board of Deputies. One year subsequently, the story of the forgery itself went public in a series of articles in the *London Times* by Phillip Grave and was eventually popularized in America in an entire book published by Herman Bernstein documenting the chronological development of the forged *Protocols*. Despite the initial press reports describing the false premise on which they were founded, the *Protocols* continued to be disseminated widely in the West establishing an important pretext for the Nazi extermination of Jews in World War II.[162]

Why is Solzhenitsyn's name associated with this calumnious document? In both the 1966 essay attributed to him and in part two of *Two Hundred Years Together*, although he does not give them credence, Solzhenitsyn does give considerable space to an analysis of *The Protocols of the Elders of Zion*, including their allusion to the advent of Communism. He discusses the anonymous author of the *Protocols* who depicted a grand design for massive restructuring of society, the creation of what would seem to be a new oligarchy, and the Jewish subjugation of millions. In Solzhenitsyn's mind, one of the more visible inconsistencies surrounding the *Protocols* is the disparity be-

---

162 See other sources for background history of *The Protocols of the Elders of Zion*, e.g., Lucien Wolf, *The Jewish Bogey and the Forged Protocols of the Learned Elders of Zion*, (London: Press Committee of the Jewish Board of Deputies, 1920); Philip Graves, „The Truth about the Protocols: A Literary Forgery," *The Times*, 16, 17, 18 Aug. 1921; Herman Bernstein, *The Truth about 'The Protocols of Zion'* (New York: Ktav Publishing House, 1971); and Norman Cohn, *Warrant for Genocide: The Myth of the Jewish World Conspiracy and the Protocols of the Elders of Zion* (London: Serif, 1996).

tween the uncivilized vernacular in which it is expressed and the deep social and religious thought it displays. *Jews in the USSR and in Future Russia* suggests the *Protocols* are a crude, near parodic rendering of a demonically subtle and well thought out plan. The article describes the *Protocols* in the following manner:

> Здесь действительно (по выпискам видно) прорисовываются контуры общественной системы, создание которой непосильно рядовой голове, вероятно и того публикатора [Нилуса], — системы к тому же динамической: сперва всеобщего расшатывания и взрыва, потом всеобщего стягивания в стройность. — Это — потрудней, чем дать проект водородной бомбы. Это действительно могло быть чьим-то гениальным выкраденным планом, это (вернее, очевидная суть этого!) — совсем не на уровне бульварной брошюры.[163]

Despite being intrigued by certain of the document's literary and semantic qualities, Solzhenitsyn is aware of the dubious spirit permeating the *Protocols*. He discusses the history surrounding Tsar Nicholas II's response to them:

> После многих безуспешных попыток «Протоколы» всё же были представлены Николаю II в 1906 году и произвели на него сильное впечатление. На полях пометы: «Какое предвидение!», «Какая точность исполнения!», «Наш Пятый год точно под их дирижёрство!», «Не может быть сомнений в их подлинности». — Но, когда правые деятели предложили проект широкого использования «Протоколов» для защиты монархии, премьер П.А. Столыпин распорядился произвести секретное расследование их происхождения. Дознание вскрыло несомненный подлог. Государь был потрясён докладом Столыпина, но написал твёрдо: «"Протоколы" изъять. Нельзя чистое дело защищать грязными способами». — И затем уж отрица-

163 "Solzhenitsyn," *Evrei v SSSR i v budushei Rossii*, 26–27.

> тельное отношение властей России к "Протоколам сионских мудрецов" проявлялось жёстко.[164]

The author of *Jews in the USSR and in Future Russia* also speaks of their style being that of a "filthy leaflet," the powerful line of thought broken, fragmented, and mixed up with malodorous incantations and psychological blunders. The interesting catch to this is that, according to Solzhenitsyn, the system drawn up is not necessarily related to Judaism *per se*. The ideas expressed could very well be plagiarized from Masonic writing; thus Jewish authorship should not necessarily be interpreted as an organic part of its design. In the suspicious minds of many Russians, however, Jews and Masons have conspired throughout history and are not always regarded separately.

Conspiracy theories have long found fertile ground in the Russian psyche. Among those is the alleged Judeo-Masonic collusion—*Zhidomasonstvo* or Jewmasonry—as it was coined in nineteenth-century Russia. Such ideas have created excellent fodder for anti-Semitic rhetoric at the turn of the twentieth century when, from an anti-Semitic perspective, Jews became the "main collaborators" of Masons in a plot for world domination. But there were historical obstacles to such ideas. Many heroes of Russian history, including General Suvorov, Marshall Kutuzov, and the Decembrists, had been Masons, as had Aleksandr Pushkin and other important writers. What is more, other incongruencies arose: Jews had undeniably limited political influence under the Tsarist regime. Nevertheless, in Imperialist Russia they made significant economic contributions, in addition to having significant representation in the October Revolution. For this reason the 1905 Revolution was not attributed to Jews alone, but to Masons as well—to *Zhidomasonstvo*, in essence.

Robert Laqueur writes insightfully of this alleged dual scheme:

> The conspiracy theory of history found its most famous expression in the infamous *Protocols of the Elders of Zion*. But the *Protocols* were apparently not deemed sufficient; a somewhat more sophisticated version of the theory was needed. Against this backdrop, anti-Masonic literature became a major industry among Russian émigrés in the 1920s

164 Solzhenitsyn, *Dvesti let vmeste*, 174–175.

> and 1930s. After 1987 these theories were disinterred by the extreme right in Russia and became part and parcel of its contemporary ideology.[165]

The controversial interpretation of the *Protocols* on the part of many anti-Semites is the presumption of an ancient conspiracy of Jews striving for world domination. At the other end of the spectrum, a relatively less extreme view denies the Jews ability to act together and presents them as separate individuals united only by common religious history. Even this second view however is not incompatible with the belief in a Jewish conspiracy. Despite writing that the *Protocols* evoked the mind of a genius, Solzhenitsyn also allegedly wrote in the 1966 article that he does not believe the document defines the social aspirations of Jews as a whole. In spite of this, Solzhenitsyn demonstrated a textual experiment in which he removed words such as "Jews," "Goyim" (Gentiles), and "conspiracy," making an interesting discovery. He remarks that the text demonstrates impressive foresight into two systems of society, the Western one and the Soviet one. While a strong thinker could possibly predict the development of the West in 1901, he asks, how could he grasp the Soviet future? In spite of these potentially insightful discoveries, Solzhenitsyn fails entirely to disarm the charge of anti-Semitic accusation when making such commentary on a document that has been a great source of Jewish racism.

---

165 Laqueur, *Black Hundred*, 39.

XII The Ambivalence of Solzhenitsyn

What is meant by Solzhenitsyn's ambivalence? The definition of "ambivalence" in a standard reference dictionary reads: "the simultaneous existence of contradictory tendencies, attitudes, or feelings on the relationship to a single object—especially the coexistence of love and hate."[166] Nathan Ackerman writes that a Jewish stereotype developing since the Christian era is one of great ambivalence: "Culturally the Jew is seen both as successful and as low class; as capitalist and as communist; as clannish and as an intruder into other people's society; as the personification of high moral and spiritual standards and as given to low primitive drives like greed and dirt; as oversexed and impotent; as male and as female; as strong and as weak; as magically omnipotent and omniscient, possessing uncanny demoniacal powers; and as being incredibly helpless, defenseless, and therefore readily attacked and destroyed."[167] A thorough examination of Solzhenitsyn's work undoubtedly exhibits duality with respect to Russian Jewry, principally with emphasis on the disparity between love and hate. For example, if Solzhenitsyn were to say: "I love Jews" or "I hate Jews," there would be evidence in his writings to support either statement.

Although much has been and still is being written of Solzhenitsyn's ostensibly adversarial view of Judaism in Russia, there is ample evidence in the man's writing and public statements that suggests his ambivalence toward the Jewish nation. It is plain that Solzhenitsyn can be very critical of Russian Jewry, especially of its pivotal involvement in the Revolution. But this is only half the story at best. As illustrated in his Jewish character sketches, Solzhenitsyn is able to write with respect and empathy for members of this nation, as well as express unexpected Judeophilia. Although many examples and voices have been cited vis-à-vis the negative quality of this ambivalence, let

---

166 Jean LaPlanche and Jean-Bertrand Pontalais, *The Language of Psychoanalysis* (London: Karnac Books, 1988), 26.

167 Nathan Ackerman and Marie Jahoda, *Anti-Semitism and Emotional Disorder: A Psychoanalytic Interpretation* (New York: Harper and Brothers, 1950), 58.

us now investigate the positive pole of Solzhenitsyn's ambivalent view of Jews. This oscillation appears to have its origin in Aleksandr's formative years when, as a youngster, he heard a story about his father Isaaky Lazhenitsyn's experience when applying for entry to the University of Kharkov. The experience was later fictionalized in *August 1914*:

> Because of his first name he was taken for a Jew, and the university had already filled its quota of Jews. Isaaki was kept waiting longingly on the very threshold of the university to which he so eagerly looked forward. He was in so much despair that he rushed to fetch his birth certificate, on which his Christian baptism was recorded. No sooner was he accepted as 'pure' than his boyish delight was soured by a bitter realization: his acceptance rested on his having proved that he did not belong to the nation through which Christ had come into the world. For a long time this unresolved problem weighed on his mind.[168]

This excerpt taken from *The Red Wheel* suggests that Solzhenitsyn began pondering the whys and wherefores of the Jewish nation at a young age. Readers and critics alike have been intrigued by this story. Perakh sees it as a "vivid episode," important in any attempt to understand Solzhenitsyn's attitude toward the Jews.[169] What is even more interesting when speaking of ambivalence is that Solzhenitsyn removed this corner of history from the 1983 Vermont-Paris edition of the novel.

Fictional characters such as Rubin, Arkhangorodsky, and Roitman from *The First Circle* depict the positive extremity of Solzhenitsyn's ambivalence; they offer a glimpse into the writer's empathy, respect, and admiration for the Jewish nation. Indeed, Solzhenitsyn feels not only a sense of brotherhood with Jews but believes they fulfill an important role in the spiritual evolution of Russia. As readers plunge deeper into Solzhenitsyn's work, they discover illuminating corners wherein the author's more veiled beliefs of Judeo-Russian fellowship are revealed. In the writer's mind there exists a mystical destiny weaving together the fates of both nationalities. In *October 1916* Solzhenitsyn discusses the Jewish Question; more specifically, that *Evrei* (the Jews) have

---

168 Solzhenitsyn, *August 1914*, 20.
169 Perakh, „Solzhenitsyn and the Jews," 13.

been "sent" to us (the Russians). Although this excerpt is a fictional dialogue between Vorotnytsev and Guchkov on the Jewish Question, it no doubt reveals views espoused by Solzhenitsyn himself. Guchkov remarks:

> *Евреи—нам посланы.* Не во всякой стране их шесть миллионов, а у нас вот есть. Зачем-то надо было, чтобы жребий русский и еврейский переплелись. Расплестутся ли когда или нет—не знаю. Чтобы злорадно назвать, как Герценштейн, пожары усадеб—'иллюминациями,' надо быть, конечно, чужой душой. То, что для нас боль, тёмные мужики не понимают, что делают, Россия жжёт и громить сама себя, а для депутата русского парламента....Ну, что о покойном...Затем, Я не стану утверждать, что евреи в целом нас любят. С другой стороной признаюсь, и Я их, в общем, больше—не люблю. Но: *они нам посланы.* И поскольку государство—наше, мы должны это переплетение решить приемлемо для всех. В Европре? –с ними обращались жёстче, чем у нас. Черта оседлости?—когда была, нисколько им не мешала засилить торговлю, промышленность и банки. И наша страна во время войны зависит—от международных еврейских денег. И в периодической печати они всесильны, да. И художественная, и театральная критика—в их руках. И невозможно пустить их в офицерство, это опасно для нашего духа. Впрочем, они туда и не стремятся. И нельзя дать им больших владений. И тем не менее это не значит, что мы должны их притеснять.[170]

"Jews have been sent to us" reads the text. These lines reflect the writer's conviction that Jews and Russians share a metaphysical bond. The origins and the purposes of such a link may not even be comprehended by the writer himself, but in his mind they are likely "made without hands." In a similar vein Solzhenitsyn speaks of the intertwined nature of Russo-Jewish relations: "Соотношение еврейской и русской судеб, переплетшихся с XVIII века, и так взрывно проявившееся в XX, — имеет какой-то глубокий исторический ключ, который мы не должны потерять и на будущее. Тут,

---

170 Solzhenitsyn, *October 1916*, 46 [Emphasis added-NL].

может быть, заложен сокровенный Замысел — и тем более мы должны стремиться к его разгадке и исполнению."[171] The reader will notice that the word "Design" (Замысел) in this quote is spelled with a capital letter, attributing Providence to the link between Jews and Russians. It is clear that the writer feels strongly about this in citing L-skii: "Я верю, что неспроста это получилось на путях России — этот контакт души иудейской и души славянской, что было тут какое-то предназначение."[172]

As mentioned, a "shadow identity" with the Jew has been suggested to lie somewhere in Solzhenitsyn's subconscious. This theory has been addressed from a psychoanalytic perspective by Daniel Rancour-Laferrière who believes there exists a surreptitious "Jewish self" in Solzhenitsyn within the construct of Freud's *Identification with the Aggressor*. Freudian theory proves problematic for many, but provocative theories from psychoanalytic study have been made on the topic of the writer's apparent "Jewish shadow." For example, this identity seems plausible whenever Solzhenitsyn explicitly or implicitly looks at something through the eyes of a Jew. In sympathy with Israeli nationalism he stated, "If I were a Jew I'd be a Zionist." This statement was made to Jewish friends in 1956 encouraging them to emigrate to Israel.[173] Certainly such words could mean conceiving a Jewish identity. According to the hypothesis, Solzhenitsyn's *Identification with the Aggressor* would have taken root as he came of age during the 1930s. Therefore, as he was subjected to mockery by his Jewish schoolmates and even religious persecution, he ultimately adopted their beliefs on the day he accepted their ideology, becoming a Young Pioneer, later a Komsomol, and even a believing Communist for a time. The God of Solzhenitsyn's past had been traded for Marx and Lenin. He had been transfigured into a Marxist on an outward level, but perhaps inwardly had gained the shadow identity of a Jew. Although one must not overlook the fact that many ethnic Russians were among the Bolshevik ranks, Solzhenitsyn's own personal views on the Judeo-Bolshevik connection lends plausibility to the idea of his adopting a new identity, even a Jewish one.

---

171 Solzhenitsyn, *Dvesti let vmeste*, 475.

172 L-skii, „Pis'mo iz Rossii," *22*, no.21 (1981), 150.

173 Grigori Svirsky, *A History of Post-War Soviet Writing: The Literature of Moral Opposition*, trans. R. Dessaix, M. Ulman (Ann Arbor: Ardis, 1981), 176; and Tatyana Babchin-Herzenburg, „Solzhenitsyn and the Jews," *Jerusalem Post* 22 (1975), 21.

Although Solzhenitsyn temporarily relinquished the Orthodox Christianity of his family for Leninism-Marxism, his years behind the prison camp wire exposed to him the truth of the totalitarian regime that had seized his homeland. Unexpectedly, the process of his re-conversion to Christianity was aided by individuals of Jewish ethnicity—Boris Gammerov and Boris Kornfeld, fellow prisoners in the Gulag. Gammerov, described as having a "Jewish tenderness of face," deeply moved Solzhenitsyn with the notion that God might exist after all. Further, Kornfeld appears in volume two of *The Gulag Archipelago* and, according to biographer Michael Scammell, is said to have enthused the writer's return to his former faith. This poignant scene occurs in a hospital room where the convalescing writer found a kindred spirit in the Jew who described his own conversion to Christianity and impressed Solzhenitsyn with the idea that he could do the same. We may conclude that these two significant changes in Solzhenitsyn's life bear witness to his tendency to "identify with the aggressor" and further deepen the notion of an ambivalent "shadow identity." In a sense, Solzhenitsyn's past rejection of God and embrace of Marxism was facilitated by Jews (as is made clear by his views of disproportionate Jewish involvement in bringing revolution to Russia); likewise his re-conversion to faith was aided by the same race. He describes his return to Christianity in the following verses:

When was it that I completely
Scattered the good seeds, one and all?
For after all I spent my boyhood
In the bright singing of Thy temples.

Bookish subtleties sparkled brightly,
Piercing my arrogant brain,
The secrets of the world were . . . in my grasp,
Life's destiny . . . as pliable as wax.

Blood seethed—and every swirl
Gleamed iridescently before me,
Without a rumble the building of my faith
Quietly crumbled within my heart.

But passing here between being and nothingness,
Stumbling and clutching at the edge,
I look behind me with a grateful tremor
Upon the life that I have lived.

Not with good judgment nor with desire
Are its twists and turns illumined.
But with the even glow of the Higher Meaning
Which became apparent to me only later on.

And now with measuring cup returned to me,
Scooping up the living water,
God of the Universe! I believe again!
Though I renounced You, You were with me![174]

Referring again to Solzhenitsyn's Gulag years, ambivalence is exhibited in his spiritual relationship with the notion of "prison." In effect, the writer's oscillating disposition toward Jews can be seen as a specific inner conflict filtered through his love/hate relationship with the labor camp years. Although he condemns the Soviet regime for its crime against humanity in creating the Gulag, as well as the West for naively supporting such a system, Solzhenitsyn wrote regarding his years in captivity, "Bless you prison for being in my life."[175] This spiritual dilemma to the Soviet prison experience reflects deep-rooted cultural Russian values which advocate the need for suffering even to the degree of masochism to pay for one's happiness. Thus wrote Dostoevsky, "There is no happiness in comfort; happiness is acquired through suffering. A man is not born for happiness. He has to pay for his happiness, and always by suffering."[176] The prison of Solzhenitsyn therefore served as both a hell and a paradise.

---

174 Aleksandr Solzhenitsyn, *The Gulag Archipelago, 1918–1956; An Experiment in Literary Investigation, II*, trans. Thomas P. Whitney (London: Fontana, 1976), 596.

175 Solzhenitsyn, *The Gulag Archipelago II*, 598.

176 Fyodor Dostoevsky, *Crime and Punishment* (New York: Modern Library, 1994), 581.

But why is there so little reference to Jewish persecution in his camp accounts? As mentioned previously, Perakh believed this omission to be the sole inauthentic detail of the account. No doubt anti-Semitism was a part of the Gulag reality. To some degree, *zeks* (заключённый, a colloquial name for a Soviet Gulag inmate) collectively are idealized in the writer's mind; they are not only a nation but the purged souls of Russia who personify the antithesis of philistinism and Western excess. Through their suffering they have become deeper, wiser, more perceptive. Therefore Solzhenitsyn did not want to attribute prejudices to the *zek*, nor did he present racism as a product of a system that, though fundamentally evil, had inadvertently allowed his nation the possibility of moral elevation. In effect, Jewish persecution by *zeks* had to be ignored in his writing, along with many other acts of prisoner informing, petty crime, and debauchery endemic throughout the Gulag nexus.

Ambivalence is manifest via the writer's self-criticism in which he sees certain of his personal attributes to be un-Russian. Felix Dreizin believed that such duality could be derived from the writer's apparent inability to live up to his own "Russian ideal." It is enlightening to unfold these various ideas against the backdrop of the writer's manifold ambivalences towards Jews. To illustrate, Solzhenitsyn is regretful of his inability to be candid, which he feels impedes achievement of his ideal person.[177] Solzhenitsyn speaks of his own excess caution, rationalization, cowardice, secrecy, and impulsiveness. Lenin and Stalin, neither of whom was fully Russian, were described as having similar traits. Further, the memoirs of his first wife, Natalia Reshetovskaia, speak of Solzhenitsyn's characteristic inhospitality: "No one ever visited us, and we visited no one."[178] In spite of Reshetovskaia's statement, he was likely justified in reclusiveness considering his "underground writer" status at the time. But traditions of hospitality are quintessentially Russian and thus memories of this time may be troubling to the writer. Further, in an episode from *The Oak and the Calf,* Solzhenitsyn recalls a time when he failed to display "Russian magnanimity" as a passenger was being abused by an inebriate on the train:

177 Solzhenitsyn, *The Oak and the Calf*, 49.

178 Natalya Reshetovskaia, *V spore so vremenom* (Moscow: Novosti Press Agency, 1975), 16.

> None of the men present tried to stop him: those who were not too old were too cautious. It would have been natural for me to jump up . . . but the precious suitcase containing all my manuscripts stood at our feet. So, in order to fulfill my duty as a Russian, I had to exercise a quite un-Russian self-restraint. I sat there, feeling ashamed and cowardly, staring at the floor while the women scolded us for our unmanliness. This was one of many times when my secret life as a writer robbed me—not always in such a humiliating way, but just as aggravatingly—of my freedom of action, my freedom to speak my mind, my freedom to stand up straight.[179]

Along the same lines, a memory of a Vlasovite being beaten by a Soviet counter-intelligence sergeant has remained before the writer's eyes as a "symbol of the Archipelago." The narrator "WAS AFRAID," he "DID AND SAID NOTHING," and "PASSED BY AS IF NOT HEARING" the Vlasovite cry for help (upper case in original).[180] Such characteristics are un-becoming of a "true Russian" and are haunting to Solzhenitsyn. What is perhaps at the crux of the issue of ambivalence, however, is not un-Russianness *per se* but the fact that being un-Russian can be interpreted as being Jewish.

At this point many critics get off the boat, feeling the crypto-Jewish "shadow identity" ascribed to the writer to be speculative nonsense. Solzhenitsyn is Russian—perhaps even *too* Russian for some. How can this be disputed further? But the issue here is not that he lashes out against such accusations of actually being a Jew, it is that he does so with such excessive vehemence. Certain scholars, including Rancour-Laferrière and Dreizin, believe that within this ambivalence is a subconscious fear of being a Jew. In the story referred to earlier of being called "Solzhenitser," he showed great anger towards critics who were convinced of his clandestine Jewishness. This could be called anti-Semitism but his emphatic denial of this and other similar statements are indicative of inner identity questions, at least from Rancour-Laferrière's point of view. Can one reject the idea of being a Jew without first considering the possibility that one is a Jew? Solzhenitsyn protests, but is it

---

179 Solzhenitsyn, *The Oak and the Calf*, 35.
180 Solzhenitsyn, *The Gulag Archipelago* , 262.

done with too much fervor? Surely a person secure in his ethnic identity would not be given to such reactions?

Additional insight into Solzhenitsyn's ambivalent shadow identity is evident in the issues surrounding his exile from Russia, but more importantly his perception of émigrés who commonly are Jews. Firstly, let us recall Solzhenitsyn's distaste for Jews seeking to leave the Soviet Union to resettle in "bountiful" America. Expressions such as "foreign (чужие) to this country" have been uttered by him about those seeking to emigrate; not only are they "alien," but the U.S. destination is also *chuzhoi*. The root *chuzh-*, which the writer uses persistently in reference to Jews or to his own exile, is a word that cannot be translated simply as the English "foreign" or "alien." Its connotation reflects further the cultural xenophobia of Russia, and thus the word has more of an edge.

As the political thaw ossified during Brezhnev's tenure, Solzhenitsyn found himself in circumstances similar to those of many Soviet Jews. He became a political émigré, a *chuzhoi*, like unto a Jew. Indeed, Scammell writes in his biography that although Solzhenitsyn harshly criticized Jews seeking rights to emigrate, the Nobel Laureate himself contemplated emigrating as many as three or four years prior to making such statements about the Jews.[181] Rancour-Laferrière states that "the two categories—émigré and Jewish—overlap for him, just as the categories "Communist" and "Jewish" overlapped in his early life experience."[182] However strange the idea of Jewish shadow identity seems, it must be considered in light of the contradictory sentiments of Solzhenitsyn.

Solzhenitsyn's latest work, *Two Hundred Years Together,* also sheds light on his ambivalent attitude towards Russian Jews. He delineates an acute distinction between pious Jews and assimilated Jews—especially those who have assimilated and were later swept up in the movement of Bolshevism. For the former he has admiration that verges on numinous reverence; the preservation of the Jewish people for more than two thousand years in Diaspora arouses amazement and respect. This is reflected in the writing of Orthodox Church Historian A. V. Kartashev, whom Solzhenitsyn quotes in the foreword of *Two Hundred Years Together* volume II:

181 Scammell, *Solzhenitsyn*, 671, 712–713.
182 Rancour-Laferrière, *Russian Literature and Psychoanalysis*, 163.

> Еврейство есть великая мировая нация. Для этого утверждения богослову и историку достаточно одного факта дарования миру Библии и порождения трёх мировых монотеистических религий. Нация, играющая огромную, непропорциональную своему статистическому меньшинству роль в мировом хозяйстве, мировой политике и мировой культуре; нация, превзошедшая всех своим национальным самоутверждением вопреки тысячелетиям рассеяния... Это хотя и не территориальная, но своего рода великая держава. Не объект филантропического сострадания, а равноправный субъект в мировом состязании великих наций.[183]

But Solzhenitsyn's feelings towards assimilated Jews remain ambivalent; he fails to comprehend why a Jew would not desire to return to Israel, the land of their forefathers. Their place in present-day Russian society seems tenuous to the writer, who advocates Slavophile visions of the Russian state. Thus, as discussed earlier, some of his difficulty lies in the fact that whether or not he is anti-Semitic, Solzhenitsyn is a genuine nationalist (though not in the extreme sense associated with Zhirinovsky and Zyuganov). As was mentioned before, most shades of Russian nationalism are not readily imbued with tolerance for Jews, partly for reasons of religion, but also because many Jews are seen as refusing to assimilate into the ethnic community of a given nation.

In *Two Hundred Years Together* Solzhenitsyn discusses a question that proved significant to world Jewry on the threshold of WWII: Does it follow that Jews should actively participate in world politics or limit themselves to Jewish politics? To this Solzhenitsyn draws on a number of Jewish writers, albeit those that fall in step with his own feelings. One such writer, Stefan Tsveig, suggests that Jews should not strive to high political office because of allegiance to Israel and the need to focus on the spiritual:

> Нашей величайшей обязанностью является самоограничение не только в политической жизни, но и во всех прочих областях...

183 A. V. Kartashev, *Gosudarstvennyi arkhiv Rossiiskoi federatsii-GARF*, Fond 5802, op. 1, ed. chron. 31, line 419–420 (1937).

> Единственная польза, единственный смысл, которые можно извлечь из трагического урока, выпавшего на долю евреев, — это их внутреннее воспитание. Лишь тогда... наши невиданные страдания имели бы хоть какой-то смысл, если бы они побудили еврея совершать не шумные, а по-настоящему великие дела.[184]

Further, Prague-born Max Brod, Jewish author and composer who discouraged Jewish assimilation into foreign nations, writes:

> Очень опасно для евреев вмешиваться в политическую жизнь других народов... Такое участие нас непременно раздавит и уничтожит». Еврей «должен ограничивать себя, воздерживаться... Воздержаться, но не отходить в сторону! Воздержаться — это значит: не стремиться к лидерству или к наградам в чужой политике, но действовать с сознанием ответственности, открыто, ясно, отнюдь не тайно, за кулисами.[185]

Needless to say, Solzhenitsyn fervently applauds the sentiments of these individuals, calling their words elevated, remarkable, and golden, for Jews and non-Jews alike.[186]

What conclusion can be drawn from ambivalence? This question does not have a lucid answer because such duality of heart often resides in the depths of an individual's subconscious and thus is not always known to the person himself. Whether Solzhenitsyn has a consciously ambivalent disposition towards Russian Jews is difficult to say. His writing, however, contains abundant evidence of ambivalence and emblematically reflects the prevalent Russian relationship with Jews.

---

184 Stefan Tsveig [Zweig], „Ne vneshnaia mishura, no vnutrennoe vospitanie," *BM* 11 (1976), 193–195.

185 Max Brod, „Lyubov' na rastoianii," *BM* 11 (1976), 198–199.

186 Solzhenitsyn, *Dvesti let vmeste* , 23.

XIII Conclusion

What is the answer to Solzhenitsyn's Jewish Question? As many questions of history, this will remain a complex subject, interpreted by disparate minds and fuelled by scores of passionate voices. In modern-day Russia Dostoevsky's statement concerning the Jewish nation continues to echo: "The final word on this great tribe has yet to be said."[187]

Solzhenitsyn, despite his great literary endeavor, feels that he has come no closer to solving the riddle posed by the role of the Jewish people in Russian history—something he summed up, in Russian ethno-philosophical style, as "a highly difficult, metaphysical question."[188]

Having expressed profuse ideas on this topic, what has been Solzhenitsyn's real contribution to the mystery of Judeo-Russian relations? From his early documentation of Gulag atrocity, to volumes of *The Red Wheel*, and finally culminating in *Two Hundred Years Together*, Aleksandr Solzhenitsyn has penetrated deep into the pivotal events that have warranted a Jewish Question in Russia. Including these issues in his canon of literature has brought him both acclamation and condemnation.

As regards anti-Semitism, readers must judge for themselves whether his works are driven by prejudice against Jews. However, determining whether or not the writer embraces anti-Semitic views is not the purpose of this thesis; rather it is to discover intricacies of post-Soviet Russo-Jewish relations via a writer who seeks to understand both sides. Through the years Solzhenitsyn has shown through word and deed that his historical perspective ascends to a higher vantage point; he possesses an uncommon objective, totally devoid of writers' vanity. Not in need of public approval, Solzhenitsyn seeks to act as a kind of referee in this protracted historical debate.[189]

Ultimately, the importance of Solzhenitsyn's sentiment is that it embodies the Russian nation's collective, volatile relationship with Judaism. The

187 Fyodor Dostoevsky quoted by Solzhenitsyn, *Dvesti let vmeste*, 16.

188 Kerstin Holm, „Will of the People," in *CDI Russian Weekly* 160 (29 June 2001).

189 Chukovskaia, „Interview with Solzhenitsyn."

writer's early trauma with Jewish schoolmates, his first and second partially Jewish wives, his ideological disenchantment with Jewish Bolsheviks, and his literary treatment of prominent Russian Jews all reflect the "Russian soul" in its historically erratic courtship with the Jewish nation. Further, Solzhenitsyn's ambivalence about Jews mirrors generations of Russia's cultural oscillation towards her Jewish population. Lastly, recent efforts made by the Russian State to ameliorate the plight of Russian Jews fall in step with Solzhenitsyn's personal desire to soothe the ethnic wounds of both nationalities.

Some questions of history have no lucid answer, but are gradually illumined through objective analysis and hindsight. The Jewish place in any Diaspora nation is complex, and Russia affords ample proof of this. As Solzhenitsyn confessed, he has not brought to light an answer to the Russian Jewish Question. In spite of this notorious modesty, his insights have the potential to create mutual resolution, understanding, and healing between the two nations.

Bibliography

„About National-Patriotic Front 'Pamiat'," http://www.pamiat.ru/about.html (as of 20 April 2005).

ACKERMAN, NATHAN, and JAHODA, MARIE, *Anti-Semitism and Emotional Disorder: A Psychoanalytic Interpretation* (New York: Harper and Brothers, 1950).

AGURSKII, M., *The Third Rome: National Bolshevism in the USSR* (Boulder: West View Press, 1987).

AIKMAN, „'Russia's Prophet in Exile,' Interview with Aleksandr Solzhenitsyn," *Time*, 134:4 (1989), 60.

„Aleksandr Solzhenitsyn obvinil svoikh kritikov v klevete," http://lenta.ru/culture/2003/10/20/solzhenitsyn (as of 20 October 2003).

ALMOG, SHMUEL, „Theorizing about Antisemitism, the Holocaust and Modernity" http://sicsa.huji.ac.il/modernity.html (as of 15 October 2003).

BABCHIN-HERZENBURG, TATIANA, „Solzhenitsyn and the Jews," *Jerusalem Post* 22 (1975), 21.

BABYONYSHEV, ALEXANDER, „review of Dvesti let vmeste (1795–1995)," http://www.fas.harvard.edu/~slavic/newsite/review/solzhenitsyn.html (as of 8 July 2003).

BARNES, CHRISTOPHER, *Boris Pasternak: A Literary Biography, Volume 2, 1928–1960* (Cambridge: Cambridge University Press, 1998).

BERDIAEV, NIKOLAI, *Khristianstvo i antisemitizm: (Religioznaia sud'ba evreistva)* (Paris: Izdanie Religiozno-Filisofskoi akademii,1938).

BERLIN, ISAIAH, „Meetings with Russian Writers in 1945 and 1956," *Personal Impressions*, (New York: The Viking Press, 1980).

BERNSTEIN, HERMAN, *The Truth about "The Protocols of Zion"* (New York: Ktav Publishing House, 1971).

BIKERMAN, IOSEF M., *K samopoznaniu evreia: Chem my byli, chem my stali, chem, my dolzhny byt'*, (Paris: n.p., 1939), 64.

BROD, MAX, „Lyubov' na rastoianii," *BM* 11 (1976), 198–199.

CARMICHAEL, JOEL, „German Money and Bolshevik Honour," *Encounter* (1974), 81–90.

CARTER, STEPHEN, *Russian Nationalism; Yesterday, Today, Tomorrow* (New York: St. Martin's Press, 1990).

CHEKHOV, ANTON, „Mire," http://www.ibiblio.org/eldritch/ac/mire.htm (as of 20 April 2005).

CHUKOVSKAIA, LYDIA, „Interview with Solzhenitsyn about 'Two Hundred Years Together,'" http://www.orthodoxytoday.org/articles/ChukovskayaSolzhenitsyn.htm (as of 1 January 2003).

COHN, NORMAN, *Warrant for Genocide: The Myth of the Jewish World Conspiracy and the Protocols of the Elders of Zion* (London: Serif, 1996).

COURTOIS, STEPHANE, et al., *The Black Book of Communism: Crimes, Terror, Repression*, trans. Jonathan Murphy (London: Harvard University Press, 1999).

DE MALLAC, GUY, *Boris Pasternak: His Life and Art* (Norman: University of Oklahoma Press, 1981).

DOSTOEVSKY, FYODOR, *Complete Works in 30 Volumes*, vol. 30 (Leningrad: Nauka, 1972).

———, *Crime and Punishment* (New York: Modern Library, 1994).

———, *Demons* (New York: A. A. Knopf, 1994).

———, *The Diary of a Writer*, trans. Boris Brasol (Salt Lake City: Peregrine Smith, Inc., 1979).

DREIZEN, FELIX, *The Russian Soul and the Jew: Essays in Literary Ethnocriticism* (Lanham: University Press of America, 1990).

DUNLOP, JOHN, „A Conversation with Dmitrii Vasiliev, the Leader of Pamiat'," *Report on the USSR*, 15 December 1989, 13–15.

———, „Russian Reactions to Solzhenitsyn's Brochure," *Report on the USSR*, 14 December 1990, 3–8.

———, *The New Russian Nationalism* (New York: Praeger, 1985).

ERICSON, EDWARD, JR., *Solzhenitsyn and the Modern World* (Washington, D.C.: Regnery Gateway, 1993).

———, *Solzhenitsyn; The Moral Vision* (Grand Rapids: William B. Eerdmans Publishing Company, 1980).

ETINGER, IAKOV, „Is There a 'Jewish Question' in Russia?," http://www.jewishpost.com/jp0610/jpn0610t.htm (as of October 2000).

FRANK, JOSEPH, „Foreword," in David Goldstein, *Dostoevsky and the Jews* (Austin: University of Texas Press, 1981).

FRIEDGUT, THEODORE, „Antisemitism and Its Opponents in the Russian Press: From Perestroika until the Present," http://sicsa.huji.ac.il/3fried.htm (as of 15 April 2003).

GIBIAN, GEORGE, „Doctor Zhivago, Russia and Leonid Pasternak's Rembrandt," in John Garrard, ed., *The Russian Novel from Pushkin to Pasternak* (New Haven: Yale University Press, 1983).

GIDWITZ, BETSY, „The Role of Politics in Contemporary Russian Antisemitism," *Jerusalem Center for Public Affairs*, no. 414 (1999), http://www.jcpa.org/jl/vp414.htm (as of 1 January 2004).

GOGOL, NIKOLAI, *Taras Bulba*, trans. Peter Constantine (New York: Random House Publishing, 2003).

GOREV, BORIS, „Russian Literature and the Jews," in *A History of Russian Jewish Literature* (Ardis: Ann Arbor, 1979).

GRAVES, PHILIP, „The Truth about the Protocols: A Literary Forgery," *The Times*, 16–18 August 1921.

GRAY, PAUL, „Russia's Prophet in Exile: Aleksandr Solzhenitsyn publishes the first volume of his epic on the Bolshevik Revolution and gives a rare account of his life in Vermont. ('The Red Wheel') (interview)," *Time*, 134:4 (1989), 56–60.

GREENE, SAM, „Fatal Heritage," http://www.tol.cz/look/CER/article.tpl?IdLanguage=1&IdPublication=14&NrIssue=46&NrSection=1&NrArticle=9083&ALStart=30 (as of 12 March 2003).

———, „Solzhenitsyn and the Jews," http://mailman.lbo-talk.org/2003/2003-March/007454.html (as of 20 April 2005).

GRENIER, RICHARD, „Solzhenitsyn and Anti-Semitism: A New Debate; Expanded Novel Prompts Dispute," *New York Times*, 13 November 1985, C21.

GUBERMAN, IGOR, *Gariki na kazhdyi den'* (Moscow: MP EMIA, 1992).

HINGLEY, RONALD, *The Russian Mind* (New York: Charles Scribner's Sons, 1977).

„History of the Jews in Russia and the Soviet Union," *Wikipedia Free Encyclopedia* http://en.wikipedia.org/wiki/History_of_the_Jews_in_Russia_and_the_Soviet_Union (as of 20 April 2005).

HITLER, ADOLF, *Mein Kampf* (Boston: Houghton Mifflin, 2001).

HOLM, KERSTIN, „Will of the People," in *CDI Russian Weekly* 160 [email newsletter] (29 June 2001) <djohnson@cdi.org>.

HOSKING, GEOFFREY, „Aleksandr Solzhenitsyn, Dvesti let vmeste, Russki Put'," in *Johnson's Russia List* [email newsletter] (5 March 2002) <davidjohnson@erols.com >.

IRBE, GEORGE, „The New Jewish Question" http://vip.latnet.lv/LPRA/g_irbe.htm (as of 18 February 2000).

„Jewish Public Organisations Say there is No More Jewish Question in Russia," http://english.pravda.ru/society/2002/06/29/31464.html (as of 29 June 2002).

IVANOVICH, S., *Semyon Yushkevich i evrei* (Jerusalem: E. Kapitaikina, 1992).

KARTASHEV, A. V., *Gosudarstvennyi arkhiv Rossiiskoi federatsii-GARF*, Fond 5802, op. 1, ed. chron. 31, line 419–420 (1937).

KAZHDAIA, VALERY, „Opus-68, ili vypadenie iz predelov tsivilizovannogo polia," www.e-slovo.ru/152/opus.htm (as of 3 June 2003).

KHATIUSHIN, VALERII, „Esli poimem—spasemsia," *Molodala Gvardia* 3 (1995).

KHEYFETS, MIKHAIL, „Pochemy zhe narody ne kayutsia?," *Vesti*, 4 June 2003.

KLIER, J. D., „Solzhenitsyn and the Kishinev Pogrom: A Slander against Russia?," *East European Jewish Affairs*, 33:1 (2003), 49–59.

KLIMOFF, ALEXIS, „Re: AIS & the Jews," *Solzhenitsyn-1* 472 [email discussion list] (5 April 2003) <solzhenitsyn-1@yahoogroups.com>.

KLIMOV, GRIGORII, *Case No. 69. On Psychological Warfare, Mad-Houses, the Third Jewmigration and the Forces of Darkness*, (Woodridge, NY: Slavia,1974).

KLINGHOFFER, DAVID, „The Changing Face of Antisemitism in Modern-Day Russia," http://www.forward.com/issues/2002/02.12.27/oped3.html (as of 27 December 2002).

KOSTYRCHENKO, GENNADY, „Iz-pod glyb veka," *Lekhaim* 133 (2000), 34–43.

KRYSKO, WLADIMIR W., *I Choose the Truth* (unpublished memoir).

L-SKII, „Pis'mo iz Rossii," *22*, no.21 (1981), 150.

LABEDZ, LEOPOLD ed., *Solzhenitsyn: A Documentary Record*, (London: Allen Lane the Penguin Press, 1970).

LAMONT, ROSETTE, „Solzhenitsyn's Nationalism," in John Dunlop et al., *Aleksandr Solzhenitsyn: Critical Essays and Documentary Materials* (New York: Nordland Publishing, 1973).

LAPLANCHE, JEAN, and PONTALAIS, JEAN-BERTRAND, *The Language of Psychoanalysis* (London: Karnac Books, 1988).

LAQUEUR, WALTER, *Black Hundred; The Rise of the Extreme Right in Russia* (New York: HarperCollins Publishers, 1993).

LENIN, VLADIMIR, *Critical Remarks on the National Question*, trans. Bernard Isaacs and Joe Fineberg, ed. Julius Katzer (vol. xx of *Collected Works, 4th Ed.*) (Moscow: Progress Publishers, 1964) http://www.marx2mao.org/Lenin/CRNQ13.html (as of 1 March 2004).

LEVIN, DANIEL, „Na krayu soblaznu:[interview]," *22*, no.1 (1978), 55.

LIMONOV, EDUARD, „Aleksandr Solzhenitsyn razrushitelen dlia Rossii," *Knizhnoe Obozrenie* 23 (1994), 23.

LOSEV, LEV, „Solzhenitsynskie Evrei," *Strelec* 1 (1989), 294–311.

———, „Velikoe budushchee," *Kontinent* 42 (1984), 315.

LOSHAK, VIKTOR, „Raskalenny vopros," *The Yonge Street Review* 149 (28 June 2001) http://www.newcanada.com/149/vopros.htm.

———, „Russians? Jews? Russian Jews?," *The Moscow News* (3 January 2003) http://english.mn.ru/english/issue.php?2002-51-9.

LVOV-ROGACHEVSKY, V., *A History of Russian Jewish Literature*, ed. and trans. Arthur Levin (Ann Arbor: Ardis Publishers, 1979).

MAHONEY, DANIEL, „Aleksandr Solzhenitsyn and the Moral Foundations of Democracy," http://www.assumption.edu/news/mag/assumagsp00/Mahoney.html (as of 1 March 2004).

———, _*Aleksandr Solzhenitsyn: The Ascent from Ideology* (Lanham: Roman & Littlefield, 2001).

———, „Solzhenitsyn on Russia's 'Jewish Question,'" *Society*, 40:1 (2002), 104–106.

———, „Solzhenitsyn, Russia, and the Jews Revisited," *Society*, 41:5 (2004), 72–82.

———, „The Continuing Relevance of Aleksandr Solzhenitsyn," *Society*, 41:1 (2003) 61–71.

MANN, STANLEY, „It Had its History," http://www.wzo.org.il/en/resources/view.asp?id=1547&subject=131 (as of 1 February 2005).

MARKISH, DAVID, „V strane moloka i miasa," *Sion* 12 (1975) 116–117.

MEDVEDEV, ZHORES, *Ten Years After Ivan Denisovich*, trans. Hilary Sternberg (New York: Vintage Books, 1974).

MONAS, SIDNEY, „Gulag points west," *Slavic Review*, 40:3 (1981), 462.

MOSSE, W. E., „Makers of the Soviet Union," *Slavonic Review* 46 (1968), 148.

NASR, ABU, „Antisemitism in Russia Today (Perspektiva)," in *Leninist-International* [email newsletter] (27 December 1999) <leninist-international@lists.econ.utah.edu>.

NICHOLSON, MICHAEL, „Effigies and Oddities," *Solzhenitsyn in Exile*, ed. J. Dunlop et al. (Stanford: Hoover Institution Press, 1985).

NORDLINGER, JAY, „Solzhenitsyn, Still: The writer and his latest challenge," http://www.nationalreview.com/ (as of 17 September 2001).

———, „Solzhenitsyn's World," *National Review*, 55:10 (2003), 25–26.

NOVOSTEI, VREMIA, „An Interview with Evgeny Satanovsky, President of the Russian Jewish Congress," in *Johnson's Russia List* [email newsletter] (21 January 2002) <davidjohnson@erols.com >.

O'DONNELL, STOJGNIEV, „The Jewish Question," http://www.jewishtribalreview.org/odonnell.htm (as of January 2003).

PASTERNAK, BORIS, *Doctor Zhivago*, trans. Max Hayward and Mania Harari (London: Collins and Harvill Press, 1958).

PEARCE, JOSEPH, *Solzhenitsyn; A Soul in Exile* (Grand Rapids: Baker Books, 1999).

PERAKH, MARK, „Solzhenitsyn and the Jews," *Midstream*, 23:6 (1977), 13.

PIPES, RICHARD, *Russia under the Bolshevik Regime* (New York: Alfred A. Knopf, 1994).

———, „Solzhenitsyn and the Jews, Revisited," http://www.benadorassociates.com/article/141 (as of 25 November 2002).

POMERANTS, G. S., „Dogmaty Polemiki," http://www.igrunov.ru/cat/vchk-cat-names-pomer-publ-dogmats.html (as of 27 March 2003).

PONARIN, EDUARD, „Aleksandr Solzhenitsyn as a Mirror of the Counter-Revolution," *Center for Strategic and International Studies*, PONARS Policy Memo 150 (2000) http://www.csis.org/ruseura/ponars/policymemos/pm_0150.pdf (as of 1 January 2004).

PONTUSO, JAMES, *Solzhenitsyn's Political Thought* (Charlottesville: University Press of Virginia, 1990).

PRIBYLOVSKII, VLADIMIR, „Oligarchs, True and False," *Russia and Eurasia Review*, 2:12 (2003) http://www.jamestown.org/publications_details.php?volume_id=16&&issue_id=624 (as of 1 November 2004).

PROKHANOV, ALEKSANDR, „Strasti po Solzhenitsynu," *Argumenty i fakty* 25 (1994), 3.

RANCOUR-LAFERRIERE, DANIEL, „Imagining Russia: Ethnic Identity and the Nationalist Mind," http://www.panorama.ru/works/patr/ir/ (as of 7 November 2003).

———, *Russian Literature and Psychoanalysis* (Amsterdam: John Benjamins Publishing, 1989).

RAYFIELD, DONALD, *Anton Chekhov; A Life* (New York: Henry Holt and Company, 1997).

REMNICK, DAVID, „Native Son," *New York Review of Books*, 38:4 (14 February 1991), 10.

RESHETOVSKAIA, NATALIA, *V spore so vremenom* (Moscow: Novosti Press Agency, 1975).

REZNIK, SEMYON, *The Nazification of Russia* (Washington D.C.: Challenge Publications, 1996).

———, *Vmeste ili vroz': Zametki na poliakh A.I. Solzhenitsyna* (Moscow: Zakharov, 2003).

ROGACHEVSKY, ANDREI, „Review of Aleksandr Solzhenitsyn, *Dvesti let vmeste (1795–1995), Part II* (Moscow, 2002)," *East European Jewish Affairs*, 33 (2003), 128–130.

ROWLEY, DAVID, „Aleksandr Solzhenitsyn and Russian nationalism," *Journal of Contemporary History*, 32:3 (1997) 321.

„Russian Jews charge Solzhenitsyn with altering history," http://www.jewishsf.com/content/2-0-/module/displaystory/story_id/16730/format/html/displaystory.html (as of 31 August 2001).

SCAMMELL, MICHAEL, *Solzhenitsyn: A Biography* (London: Paladin Grafton Books, 1984).

SCHAPIRO, LEONARD, *Times Literary Supplement* 10 (November 1978), 1301.

SHAMIR, ISRAEL, „Evreskie ruchi v russkom more," *Zavtra*, 7:83 (2003) http://www.zavtra.ru/cgi/veil/data/denlit/083/32.html (as of 1 February 2004).

———, „The Elders of Zion and the Masters of Discourse," http://www.rense.com/general32/elders.htm (as of 11 September 2003).

SHENFIELD, STEPHEN, *Russian Fascism: Traditions, Tendencies, Movements* (Armonk: M.E. Sharpe, 2001).

SHIMANOV, GENADI, „O tainoi prirode kapitalizma," *Veche* (1991), 10.

SHLAPENTOKH, DMITRI, „The Fate of the Jews in Post-Soviet Russia," *The World and I*, 19:4 (2000), 279–295.

SHNEERSON, MARIA, „Arguments about Solzhenitsyn," *Novy amerikanets* 111 (1982), 23.

SINIAVSKY, ANDREI, and ANDREIEV CARLISLE, OLGA, „Solzhenitsyn and Russian Nationalism: An Interview with Andrei Siniavsky," *New York*

Review of Books, 26:18 (1979) http://www.nybooks.com/articles/article-preview?article_id=7611 (as of 1 March 2004).

SNIEGOSKY, STEPHEN, „What does Podhoretz mean by 'anti-Semitism'?," http://www.thornwalker.com/ditch/snieg9.htm (as of 29 November 1999).

SOLOV'ËV, VLADIMIR, *Natsional'nyi vopros v Rossii. Vypusk pervyi, 1838-1888, T.5* (Brussel: Fototipicheskoe vosproizvedenie, 1966).

SOLZHENITSYN, ALEKSANDR, *August 1914*, trans. M. Glenny (New York: Bantam, 1974).

———, *Cancer Ward*, trans. Rebecca Frank (New York: Modern Library, 1983).

———, „*Dvesti let vmeste*," http://sila.by.ru (as of 20 April 2005).

———, *Dvesti let vmeste 1795–1995, chast' II* (Moscow: Russky Put', 2002).

"SOLZHENITSYN, ALEKSANDR," *Evrei v SSSR i v budushei Rossii* (Slaviansk: Pechatnyi dvor, 2000).

———, *Lenin in Zurich*, trans. Harry Willets (New York: Farar, Straus and Giroux, 1976).

———, *Oktiabr' 1916* (Paris: YMCA Press, 1984).

———, *Skvoz' Chad* (Paris: YMCA Press, 1979).

———, *The First Circle*, trans. Thomas P. Whitney (New York: Harper & Row, 1968).

———, *The Gulag Archipelago, 1918–1956; An Experiment in Literary Investigation, I*, trans. Thomas P. Whitney (Boulder: Westview Press, 1998).

———, *The Gulag Archipelago, 1918–1956; An Experiment in Literary Investigation, II*, trans. Thomas P. Whitney (London: Fontana, 1976).

———, *The Gulag Archipelago, 1918–1956; An Experiment in Literary Investigation, V-VII*, trans. Thomas P. Whitney (New York: Harper & Row, 1976).

———, *The Oak and the Calf: Sketches of Literary Life in the Soviet Union*, trans. Harry Willetts (New York: Harper & Row, 1979).

———, *Rebuilding Russia; Reflections and Tentative Proposals*, trans. Alexis Klimoff (New York: Farrar, Straus and Giroux: 1991).

———, *'The Russian Question' At the End of the Twentieth Century*, trans. Ermolai Solzhenitsyn (New York: Farrar, Straus and Giroux: 1995).

———, *Warning to the West* (New York: Harper & Row, 1986).

SOLZHENITSYN, ALEKSANDR, and KLIMOFF, ALEXIS, *The Mortal Danger: How Misconceptions about Russia Imperil America* (New York: Harper & Row, 1980).

SOLZHENITSYN, ALEKSANDR, with Mikhail Agurskii et al. *From Under the Rubble*, trans. A. M. Brock et al. (Washington D.C.: Regnery, 1981).

„Solzhenitsyn in Zurich—an interview," *Encounter* 271 (1976), 11.

„Solzhenitsyn: Interview with the Moscow News," *Moscow News* 25 (2001).

„Solzhenitsyn: Nyneshnaia kleveta na menia polnost'iu tozhdestvenna prezhnei, gebistskoi," http://lenta.ru/culture/2003/10/22/solzhenitsyn (as of 22 October 2003).

„Solzhenitsyn: Russia Rooted in Rot," http://www.newsmax.com/articles/?a=2000/5/14/172120 (as of 16 May 2000).

SUTTER, THOMAS, „What's National-Bolshevism? Philosophical Basis & Metaphysic Heritage [Summary]," http://www.bolsheviks.org/DOCUMENTS/WHAT.htm (as of 20 April 2005).

SVIRSKI, GRIGORI, *A History of Post-War Soviet Writing: The Literature of Moral Opposition*, trans. R. Dessaix and M. Ulman (Ann Arbor: Ardis, 1981).

TERTS, ABRAM (Andrei Siniavsky), „Literaturnyi protsess v Rossii," *Kontinent* 1 (1974), 183.

THOMAS, D. M., *Alexander Solzhenitsyn: A Century in His Life* (New York: St. Martin's Press, 1998).

TSVEIG [ZWEIG], STEFAN, „Ne vneshniaia mishura, no vnutrennoe vospitanie," *BM* 11 (1976), 193–195.

UNGVARI, TAMAS, *The "Jewish Question" in Europe; The Case of Hungary* (New York: Columbia University Press, 2000).

UNION OF COUNCILS FOR JEWS IN THE FORMER SOVIET UNION, „Antisemitism in Russia, 1995–97," http://www.fsumonitor.com/stories/asem1rus2.shtml (as of 20 April 2005).

VAYMAN, NAUM, „Ne sotvori sebe kumira," *Vesti*, 26 June 2003.

———, „Perepiska iz dvukh uglov," *Vesti*, 10 April 2003.

WALSH, NICK PATON, „Solzhenitsyn breaks last taboo of the revolution," http://www.guardian.co.uk/russia/article/0,2763,881984,00.html (as of 25 January 2003).

WARREN, MARCUS, „Solzhenitsyn tries to heal Jewish wounds:[Daily Edition]," *Jerusalem Post*, 21 June 2001.

WOLF, LUCIEN, *The Jewish Bogey and the Forged Protocols of the Learned Elders of Zion* (London: Press Committee of the Jewish Board of Deputies, 1920).

YOUNG, C., „The anti-Semitism of Alexander Solzhenitsyn," *Reason*, 36:1 (2004), 20–21.

Index

SOVIET AND POST-SOVIET POLITICS AND SOCIETY

Edited by Dr. Andreas Umland

ISSN 1614-3515

1 *Андреас Умланд (ред.)*
Воплощение Европейской конвенции по правам человека в России
Философские, юридические и эмпирические исследования
ISBN 3-89821-387-0

2 *Christian Wipperfürth*
Russland – ein vertrauenswürdiger Partner?
Grundlagen, Hintergründe und Praxis gegenwärtiger russischer Außenpolitik
Mit einem Vorwort von Heinz Timmermann
ISBN 3-89821-401-X

3 *Manja Hussner*
Die Übernahme internationalen Rechts in die russische und deutsche Rechtsordnung
Eine vergleichende Analyse zur Völkerrechtsfreundlichkeit der Verfassungen der Russländischen Föderation und der Bundesrepublik Deutschland
Mit einem Vorwort von Rainer Arnold
ISBN 3-89821-438-9

4 *Matthew Tejada*
Bulgaria's Democratic Consolidation and the Kozloduy Nuclear Power Plant (KNPP)
The Unattainability of Closure
With a foreword by Richard J. Crampton
ISBN 3-89821-439-7

5 *Марк Григорьевич Меерович*
Квадратные метры, определяющие сознание
Государственная жилищная политика в СССР. 1921 – 1941 гг
ISBN 3-89821-474-5

6 *Andrei P. Tsygankov, Pavel A.Tsygankov (Eds.)*
New Directions in Russian International Studies
ISBN 3-89821-422-2

7 *Марк Григорьевич Меерович*
Как власть народ к труду приучала
Жилище в СССР – средство управления людьми. 1917 – 1941 гг.
С предисловием Елены Осокиной
ISBN 3-89821-495-8

8 *David J. Galbreath*
Nation-Building and Minority Politics in Post-Socialist States
Interests, Influence and Identities in Estonia and Latvia
With a foreword by David J. Smith
ISBN 3-89821-467-2

9 *Алексей Юрьевич Безугольный*
Народы Кавказа в Вооруженных силах СССР в годы Великой Отечественной войны 1941-1945 гг.
С предисловием Николая Бугая
ISBN 3-89821-475-3

10 *Вячеслав Лихачев и Владимир Прибыловский (ред.)*
Русское Национальное Единство, 1990-2000. В 2-х томах
ISBN 3-89821-523-7

11 *Николай Бугай (ред.)*
Народы стран Балтии в условиях сталинизма (1940-е – 1950-е годы)
Документированная история
ISBN 3-89821-525-3

12 *Ingmar Bredies (Hrsg.)*
Zur Anatomie der Orange Revolution in der Ukraine
Wechsel des Elitenregimes oder Triumph des Parlamentarismus?
ISBN 3-89821-524-5

13 *Anastasia V. Mitrofanova*
The Politicization of Russian Orthodoxy
Actors and Ideas
With a foreword by William C. Gay
ISBN 3-89821-481-8

14 *Nathan D. Larson*
Alexander Solzhenitsyn and the Russo-Jewish Question
ISBN 3-89821-483-4

15 *Guido Houben*
Kulturpolitik und Ethnizität
Staatliche Kunstförderung im Russland der neunziger Jahre
Mit einem Vorwort von Gert Weisskirchen
ISBN 3-89821-542-3

16 *Leonid Luks*
Der russische „Sonderweg"?
Aufsätze zur neuesten Geschichte Russlands im europäischen Kontext
ISBN 3-89821-496-6

17 *Евгений Мороз*
История «Мёртвой воды» – от страшной сказки к большой политике
Политическое неоязычество в постсоветской России
ISBN 3-89821-551-2

18 *Александр Верховский и Галина Кожевникова (ред.)*
Этническая и религиозная интолерантность в российских СМИ
Результаты мониторинга 2001-2004 гг.
ISBN 3-89821-569-5

19 *Christian Ganzer*
Sowjetisches Erbe und ukrainische Nation
Das Museum der Geschichte des Zaporoger Kosakentums auf der Insel Chortycja
Mit einem Vorwort von Frank Golczewski
ISBN 3-89821-504-0

20 *Эльза-Баир Гучинова*
Помнить нельзя забыть
Антропология депортационной травмы калмыков
С предисловием Кэролайн Хамфри
ISBN 3-89821-506-7

21 *Юлия Лидерман*
Мотивы «проверки» и «испытания» в постсоветской культуре
Советское прошлое в российском кинематографе 1990-х годов
С предисловием Евгения Марголита
ISBN 3-89821-511-3

22 *Tanya Lokshina, Ray Thomas, Mary Mayer (Eds.)*
The Imposition of a Fake Political Settlement in the Northern Caucasus
The 2003 Chechen Presidential Election
ISBN 3-89821-436-2

23 *Timothy McCajor Hall, Rosie Read (Eds.)*
Changes in the Heart of Europe
Recent Ethnographies of Czechs, Slovaks, Roma, and Sorbs
With an afterword by Zdeněk Salzmann
ISBN 3-89821-606-3

24 *Christian Autengruber*
Die politischen Parteien in Bulgarien und Rumänien
Eine vergleichende Analyse seit Beginn der 90er Jahre
Mit einem Vorwort von Dorothée de Nève
ISBN 3-89821-476-1

25 *Annette Freyberg-Inan with Radu Cristescu*
The Ghosts in Our Classrooms, or: John Dewey Meets Ceauşescu
The Promise and the Failures of Civic Education in Romania
ISBN 3-89821-416-8

26 *John B. Dunlop*
The 2002 Dubrovka and 2004 Beslan Hostage Crises
A Critique of Russian Counter-Terrorism
With a foreword by Donald N. Jensen
ISBN 3-89821-608-X

27 *Peter Koller*
Das touristische Potenzial von Kam''janec'–Podil's'kyj
Eine fremdenverkehrsgeographische Untersuchung der Zukunftsperspektiven und Maßnahmenplanung zur Destinationsentwicklung des „ukrainischen Rothenburg"
Mit einem Vorwort von Kristiane Klemm
ISBN 3-89821-640-3

28 *Françoise Daucé, Elisabeth Sieca-Kozlowski (Eds.)*
Dedovshchina in the Post-Soviet Military
Hazing of Russian Army Conscripts in a Comparative Perspective
With a foreword by Dale Herspring
ISBN 3-89821-616-0

29 *Florian Strasser*
Zivilgesellschaftliche Einflüsse auf die Orange Revolution
Die gewaltlose Massenbewegung und die ukrainische Wahlkrise 2004
Mit einem Vorwort von Egbert Jahn
ISBN 3-89821-648-9

30 *Rebecca S. Katz*
The Georgian Regime Crisis of 2003-2004
A Case Study in Post-Soviet Media Representation of Politics, Crime and Corruption
ISBN 3-89821-413-3

31 *Vladimir Kantor*
Willkür oder Freiheit
Beiträge zur russischen Geschichtsphilosophie
Ediert von Dagmar Herrmann sowie mit einem Vorwort versehen von Leonid Luks
ISBN 3-89821-589-X

32 *Laura A. Victoir*
The Russian Land Estate Today
A Case Study of Cultural Politics in Post-Soviet Russia
With a foreword by Priscilla Roosevelt
ISBN 3-89821-426-5

33 *Ivan Katchanovski*
Cleft Countries
Regional Political Divisions and Cultures in Post-Soviet Ukraine and Moldova
With a foreword by Francis Fukuyama
ISBN 3-89821-558-X

34 *Florian Mühlfried*
Postsowjetische Feiern
Das Georgische Bankett im Wandel
Mit einem Vorwort von Kevin Tuite
ISBN 3-89821-601-2

35 *Roger Griffin, Werner Loh, Andreas Umland (Eds.)*
Fascism Past and Present, West and East
An International Debate on Concepts and Cases in the Comparative Study of the Extreme Right
With an afterword by Walter Laqueur
ISBN 3-89821-674-8

36 *Sebastian Schlegel*
Der „Weiße Archipel“
Sowjetische Atomstädte 1945-1991
Mit einem Geleitwort von Thomas Bohn
ISBN 3-89821-679-9

37 *Vyacheslav Likhachev*
Political Anti-Semitism in Post-Soviet Russia
Actors and Ideas in 1991-2003
Edited and translated from Russian by Eugene Veklerov
ISBN 3-89821-529-6

38 *Josette Baer (Ed.)*
Preparing Liberty in Central Europe
Political Texts from the Spring of Nations 1848 to the Spring of Prague 1968
With a foreword by Zdeněk V. David
ISBN 3-89821-546-6

39 *Михаил Лукьянов*
Российский консерватизм и реформа, 1907-1914
С предисловием Марка Д. Стейнберга
ISBN 3-89821-503-2

40 *Nicola Melloni*
Market Without Economy
The 1998 Russian Financial Crisis
With a foreword by Eiji Furukawa
ISBN 3-89821-407-9

41 *Dmitrij Chmelnizki*
Die Architektur Stalins
Bd. 1: Studien zu Ideologie und Stil
Bd. 2: Bilddokumentation
Mit einem Vorwort von Bruno Flierl
ISBN 3-89821-515-6

42 *Katja Yafimava*
Post-Soviet Russian-Belarussian Relationships
The Role of Gas Transit Pipelines
With a foreword by Jonathan P. Stern
ISBN 3-89821-655-1

43 *Boris Chavkin*
Verflechtungen der deutschen und russischen Zeitgeschichte
Aufsätze und Archivfunde zu den Beziehungen Deutschlands und der Sowjetunion von 1917 bis 1991
Ediert von Markus Edlinger sowie mit einem Vorwort versehen von Leonid Luks
ISBN 3-89821-756-6

44 *Anastasija Grynenko in Zusammenarbeit mit Claudia Dathe*
Die Terminologie des Gerichtswesens der Ukraine und Deutschlands im Vergleich
Eine übersetzungswissenschaftliche Analyse juristischer Fachbegriffe im Deutschen, Ukrainischen und Russischen
Mit einem Vorwort von Ulrich Hartmann
ISBN 3-89821-691-8

45 *Anton Burkov*
The Impact of the European Convention on Human Rights on Russian Law
Legislation and Application in 1996-2006
With a foreword by Françoise Hampson
ISBN 978-3-89821-639-5

46 *Stina Torjesen, Indra Overland (Eds.)*
International Election Observers in Post-Soviet Azerbaijan
Geopolitical Pawns or Agents of Change?
ISBN 978-3-89821-743-9

47 *Taras Kuzio*
Ukraine – Crimea – Russia
Triangle of Conflict
ISBN 978-3-89821-761-3

48 *Claudia Šabić*
"Ich erinnere mich nicht, aber L'viv!"
Zur Funktion kultureller Faktoren für die Institutionalisierung und Entwicklung einer ukrainischen Region
Mit einem Vorwort von Melanie Tatur
ISBN 978-3-89821-752-1

49 *Marlies Bilz*
Tatarstan in der Transformation
Nationaler Diskurs und Politische Praxis 1988-1994
Mit einem Vorwort von Frank Golczewski
ISBN 978-3-89821-722-4

50 *Марлен Ларюэль (ред.)*
Современные интерпретации русского национализма
ISBN 978-3-89821-795-8

51 *Sonja Schüler*
Die ethnische Dimension der Armut
Roma im postsozialistischen Rumänien
Mit einem Vorwort von Anton Sterbling
ISBN 978-3-89821-776-7

52 *Галина Кожевникова*
Радикальный национализм в России и противодействие ему
Сборник докладов Центра «Сова» за 2004-2007 гг.
С предисловием Александра Верховского
ISBN 978-3-89821-721-7

53 *Галина Кожевникова и Владимир Прибыловский*
Российская власть в биографиях I
Высшие должностные лица РФ в 2004 г.
ISBN 978-3-89821-796-5

54 *Галина Кожевникова и Владимир Прибыловский*
Российская власть в биографиях II
Члены Правительства РФ в 2004 г.
ISBN 978-3-89821-797-2

55 *Галина Кожевникова и Владимир Прибыловский*
Российская власть в биографиях III
Руководители федеральных служб и агентств РФ в 2004 г.
ISBN 978-3-89821-798-9

56 *Ileana Petroniu*
Privatisierung in Transformationsökonomien
Determinanten der Restrukturierungs-Bereitschaft am Beispiel Polens, Rumäniens und der Ukraine
Mit einem Vorwort von Rainer W. Schäfer
ISBN 978-3-89821-790-3

57 *Christian Wipperfürth*
Russland und seine GUS-Nachbarn
Hintergründe, aktuelle Entwicklungen und Konflikte in einer ressourcenreichen Region
ISBN 978-3-89821-801-6

58 *Togzhan Kassenova*
From Antagonism to Partnership
The Uneasy Path of the U.S.-Russian Cooperative Threat Reduction
With a foreword by Christoph Bluth
ISBN 978-3-89821-707-1

59 *Alexander Höllwerth*
Das sakrale eurasische Imperium des Aleksandr Dugin
Eine Diskursanalyse zum postsowjetischen russischen Rechtsextremismus
Mit einem Vorwort von Dirk Uffelmann
ISBN 978-3-89821-813-9

60 *Олег Рябов*
«Россия-Матушка»
Национализм, гендер и война в России XX века
С предисловием Елены Гощило
ISBN 978-3-89821-487-2

61 *Ivan Maistrenko*
Borot'bism
A Chapter in the History of the Ukrainian Revolution
With a new introduction by Chris Ford
Translated by George S. N. Luckyj with the assistance of Ivan L. Rudnytsky
ISBN 978-3-89821-697-5

62 *Maryna Romanets*
Anamorphosic Texts and Reconfigured Visions
Improvised Traditions in Contemporary Ukrainian and Irish Literature
ISBN 978-3-89821-576-3

63 *Paul D'Anieri and Taras Kuzio (Eds.)*
Aspects of the Orange Revolution I
Democratization and Elections in Post-Communist Ukraine
ISBN 978-3-89821-698-2

64 *Bohdan Harasymiw in collaboration with Oleh S. Ilnytzkyj (Eds.)*
Aspects of the Orange Revolution II
Information and Manipulation Strategies in the 2004 Ukrainian Presidential Elections
ISBN 978-3-89821-699-9

65 *Ingmar Bredies, Andreas Umland and Valentin Yakushik (Eds.)*
Aspects of the Orange Revolution III
The Context and Dynamics of the 2004 Ukrainian Presidential Elections
ISBN 978-3-89821-803-0

66 *Ingmar Bredies, Andreas Umland and Valentin Yakushik (Eds.)*
Aspects of the Orange Revolution IV
Foreign Assistance and Civic Action in the 2004 Ukrainian Presidential Elections
ISBN 978-3-89821-808-5

67 *Ingmar Bredies, Andreas Umland and Valentin Yakushik (Eds.)*
Aspects of the Orange Revolution V
Institutional Observation Reports on the 2004 Ukrainian Presidential Elections
ISBN 978-3-89821-809-2

68 *Taras Kuzio (Ed.)*
Aspects of the Orange Revolution VI
Post-Communist Democratic Revolutions in Comparative Perspective
ISBN 978-3-89821-820-7

69 *Tim Bohse*
Autoritarismus statt Selbstverwaltung
Die Transformation der kommunalen Politik in der Stadt Kaliningrad 1990-2005
Mit einem Geleitwort von Stefan Troebst
ISBN 978-3-89821-782-8

70 *David Rupp*
Die Rußländische Föderation und die russischsprachige Minderheit in Lettland
Eine Fallstudie zur Anwaltspolitik Moskaus gegenüber den russophonen Minderheiten im „Nahen Ausland" von 1991 bis 2002
Mit einem Vorwort von Helmut Wagner
ISBN 978-3-89821-778-1

71 *Taras Kuzio*
Theoretical and Comparative Perspectives on Nationalism
New Directions in Cross-Cultural and Post-Communist Studies
With a foreword by Paul Robert Magocsi
ISBN 978-3-89821-815-3

72 *Christine Teichmann*
Die Hochschultransformation im heutigen Osteuropa
Kontinuität und Wandel bei der Entwicklung des postkommunistischen Universitätswesens
Mit einem Vorwort von Oskar Anweiler
ISBN 978-3-89821-842-9

73 *Julia Kusznir*
Der politische Einfluss von Wirtschaftseliten in russischen Regionen
Eine Analyse am Beispiel der Erdöl- und Erdgasindustrie, 1992-2005
Mit einem Vorwort von Wolfgang Eichwede
ISBN 978-3-89821-821-4

74 *Alena Vysotskaya*
Russland, Belarus und die EU-Osterweiterung
Zur Minderheitenfrage und zum Problem der Freizügigkeit des Personenverkehrs
Mit einem Vorwort von Katlijn Malfliet
ISBN 978-3-89821-822-1

75 *Heiko Pleines (Hrsg.)*
Corporate Governance in post-sozialistischen Volkswirtschaften
ISBN 978-3-89821-766-8

76 *Stefan Ihrig*
Wer sind die Moldawier?
Rumänismus versus Moldowanismus in Historiographie und Schulbüchern der Republik Moldova, 1991-2006
Mit einem Vorwort von Holm Sundhaussen
ISBN 978-3-89821-466-7

77 *Galina Kozhevnikova in collaboration with Alexander Verkhovsky and Eugene Veklerov*
Ultra-Nationalism and Hate Crimes in Contemporary Russia
The 2004-2006 Annual Reports of Moscow's SOVA Center
With a foreword by Stephen D. Shenfield
ISBN 978-3-89821-868-9

78 *Florian Küchler*
The Role of the European Union in Moldova's Transnistria Conflict
With a foreword by Christopher Hill
ISBN 978-3-89821-850-4

79 *Bernd Rechel*
The Long Way Back to Europe
Minority Protection in Bulgaria
With a foreword by Richard Crampton
ISBN 978-3-89821-863-4

80 *Peter W. Rodgers*
Nation, Region and History in Post-Communist Transitions
Identity Politics in Ukraine, 1991-2006
With a foreword by Vera Tolz
ISBN 978-3-89821-903-7

81 *Stephanie Solywoda*
The Life and Work of Semen L. Frank
A Study of Russian Religious Philosophy
With a foreword by Philip Walters
ISBN 978-3-89821-457-5

82 *Vera Sokolova*
Cultural Politics of Ethnicity
Discourses on Roma in Communist Czechoslovakia
ISBN 978-3-89821-864-1

83 *Natalya Shevchik Ketenci*
Kazakhstani Enterprises in Transition
The Role of Historical Regional Development in Kazakhstan's Post-Soviet Economic Transformation
ISBN 978-3-89821-831-3

84 *Martin Malek, Anna Schor-Tschudnowskaja (Hrsg.)*
Europa im Tschetschenienkrieg
Zwischen politischer Ohnmacht und Gleichgültigkeit
Mit einem Vorwort von Lipchan Basajewa
ISBN 978-3-89821-676-0

85 *Stefan Meister*
Das postsowjetische Universitätswesen zwischen nationalem und internationalem Wandel
Die Entwicklung der regionalen Hochschule in Russland als Gradmesser der Systemtransformation
Mit einem Vorwort von Joan DeBardeleben
ISBN 978-3-89821-891-7

86 *Konstantin Sheiko in collaboration with Stephen Brown*
Nationalist Imaginings of the Russian Past
Anatolii Fomenko and the Rise of Alternative History in Post-Communist Russia
With a foreword by Donald Ostrowski
ISBN 978-3-89821-915-0

87 *Sabine Jenni*
Wie stark ist das „Einige Russland"?
Zur Parteibindung der Eliten und zum Wahlerfolg der Machtpartei im Dezember 2007
Mit einem Vorwort von Klaus Armingeon
ISBN 978-3-89821-961-7

88 *Thomas Borén*
Meeting-Places of Transformation
Urban Identity, Spatial Representations and Local Politics in Post-Soviet St Petersburg
ISBN 978-3-89821-739-2

89 *Aygul Ashirova*
Stalinismus und Stalin-Kult in Zentralasien
Turkmenistan 1924-1953
Mit einem Vorwort von Leonid Luks
ISBN 978-3-89821-987-7

90 *Leonid Luks*
Freiheit oder imperiale Größe?
Essays zu einem russischen Dilemma
ISBN 978-3-8382-0011-8

91 *Christopher Gilley*
The 'Change of Signposts' in the Ukrainian Emigration
A Contribution to the History of Sovietophilism in the 1920s
With a foreword by Frank Golczewski
ISBN 978-3-89821-965-5

92 *Philipp Casula, Jeronim Perovic (Eds.)*
Identities and Politics During the Putin Presidency
The Discursive Foundations of Russia's Stability
With a foreword by Heiko Haumann
ISBN 978-3-8382-0015-6

93 *Marcel Viëtor*
Europa und die Frage nach seinen Grenzen im Osten
Zur Konstruktion ‚europäischer Identität' in Geschichte und Gegenwart
Mit einem Vorwort von Albrecht Lehmann
ISBN 978-3-8382-0045-3

94 *Ben Hellman, Andrei Rogachevskii*
Filming the Unfilmable
Casper Wrede's 'One Day in the Life of Ivan Denisovich'
ISBN 978-3-8382-0044-6

95 *Eva Fuchslocher*
Vaterland, Sprache, Glaube
Orthodoxie und Nationenbildung am Beispiel Georgiens
Mit einem Vorwort von Christina von Braun
ISBN 978-3-89821-884-9

96 *Vladimir Kantor*
Das Westlertum und der Weg Russlands
Zur Entwicklung der russischen Literatur und Philosophie
Ediert von Dagmar Herrmann
Mit einem Beitrag von Nikolaus Lobkowicz
ISBN 978-3-8382-0102-3

97 *Kamran Musayev*
Die postsowjetische Transformation im Baltikum und Südkaukasus
Eine vergleichende Untersuchung der politischen Entwicklung Lettlands und Aserbaidschans 1985-2009
Mit einem Vorwort von Leonid Luks
Ediert von Sandro Henschel
ISBN 978-3-8382-0103-0

98 *Tatiana Zhurzhenko*
Borderlands into Bordered Lands
Geopolitics of Identity in Post-Soviet Ukraine
With a foreword by Dieter Segert
ISBN 978-3-8382-0042-2

99 *Кирилл Галушко, Лидия Смола (ред.)*
Пределы падения – варианты украинского будущего
Аналитико-прогностические исследования
ISBN 978-3-8382-0148-1

100 *Michael Minkenberg (ed.)*
Historical Legacies and the Radical Right in Post-Cold War Central and Eastern Europe
With an afterword by Sabrina P. Ramet
ISBN 978-3-8382-0124-5

101 *David-Emil Wickström*
"Okna otkroi!" – "Open the Windows!"
Transcultural Flows and Identity Politics in the St. Petersburg Popular Music Scene
With a foreword by Yngvar B. Steinholt
ISBN 978-3-8382-0100-9

102 *Eva Zabka*
Eine neue „Zeit der Wirren"?
Der spät- und postsowjetische Systemwandel 1985-2000 im Spiegel russischer gesellschaftspolitischer Diskurse
Mit einem Vorwort von Margareta Mommsen
ISBN 978-3-8382-0161-0

103 *Ulrike Ziemer*
Ethnic Belonging, Gender and Cultural Practices
Youth Identitites in Contemporary Russia
With a foreword by Anoop Nayak
ISBN 978-3-8382-0152-8

104 *Ksenia Chepikova*
‚Einiges Russland' - eine zweite KPdSU?
Aspekte der Identitätskonstruktion einer postsowjetischen „Partei der Macht“
Mit einem Vorwort von Torsten Oppelland
ISBN 978-3-8382-0311-9

105 *Леонид Люкс*
Западничество или евразийство? Демократия или идеократия?
Сборник статей об исторических дилеммах России
С предисловием Владимира Кантора
ISBN 978-3-8382-0211-2

106 *Anna Dost*
Das russische Verfassungsrecht auf dem Weg zum Föderalismus und zurück
Zum Konflikt von Rechtsnormen und -wirklichkeit in der Russländischen Föderation von 1991 bis 2009
Mit einem Vorwort von Alexander Blankenagel
ISBN 978-3-8382-0292-1

107 *Philipp Herzog*
Sozialistische Völkerfreundschaft, nationaler Widerstand oder harmloser Zeitvertreib?
Zur politischen Funktion der Volkskunst im sowjetischen Estland
Mit einem Vorwort von Andreas Kappeler
ISBN 978-3-8382-0216-7

108 *Marlène Laruelle (ed.)*
Russian Nationalism, Foreign Policy, and Identity Debates in Putin's Russia
New Ideological Patterns after the Orange Revolution
ISBN 978-3-8382-0325-6

109 *Michail Logvinov*
Russlands Kampf gegen den internationalen Terrorismus
Eine kritische Bestandsaufnahme des Bekämpfungsansatzes
Mit einem Geleitwort von Hans-Henning Schröder und einem Vorwort von Eckhard Jesse
ISBN 978-3-8382-0329-4

110 *John B. Dunlop*
The Moscow Bombings of September 1999
Examinations of Russian Terrorist Attacks at the Onset of Vladimir Putin's Rule
ISBN 978-3-8382-0388-1

111 *Андрей А. Ковалёв*
Свидетельство из-за кулис российской политики I
Можно ли делать добро из зла? (Воспоминания и размышления о последних советских и первых послесоветских годах)
With a foreword by Peter Reddaway
ISBN 978-3-8382-0302-7

112 *Андрей А. Ковалёв*
Свидетельство из-за кулис российской политики II
Угроза для себя и окружающих (Наблюдения и предостережения относительно происходящего после 2000 г.)
ISBN 978-3-8382-0303-4

113 *Bernd Kappenberg*
Zeichen setzen für Europa
Der Gebrauch europäischer lateinischer Sonderzeichen in der deutschen Öffentlichkeit
Mit einem Vorwort von Peter Schlobinski
ISBN 978-3-89821-749-1

114 *Ivo Mijnssen*
The Quest for an Ideal Youth in Putin's Russia I
Back to Our Future! History, Modernity and Patriotism according to *Nashi*, 2005-2012
With a foreword by Jeronim Perović
ISBN 978-3-8382-0368-3

115 *Jussi Lassila*
The Quest for an Ideal Youth in Putin's Russia II
The Search for Distinctive Conformism in the Political Communication of *Nashi*, 2005-2009
With a foreword by Kirill Postoutenko
ISBN 978-3-8382-0415-4

116 *Valerio Trabandt*
Neue Nachbarn, gute Nachbarschaft?
Die EU als internationaler Akteur am Beispiel ihrer Demokratieförderung in Belarus und der Ukraine 2004-2009
Mit einem Vorwort von Jutta Joachim
ISBN 978-3-8382-0437-6

117 *Fabian Pfeiffer*
Estlands Außen- und Sicherheitspolitik I
Der estnische Atlantizismus nach der wiedererlangten Unabhängigkeit 1991-2004
Mit einem Vorwort von Helmut Hubel
ISBN 978-3-8382-0127-6

118 *Jana Podßuweit*
Estlands Außen- und Sicherheitspolitik II
Handlungsoptionen eines Kleinstaates im Rahmen seiner EU-Mitgliedschaft (2004-2008)
Mit einem Vorwort von Helmut Hubel
ISBN 978-3-8382-0440-6

119 *Karin Pointner*
Estlands Außen- und Sicherheitspolitik III
Eine gedächtnispolitische Analyse estnischer Entwicklungskooperation 2006-2010
Mit einem Vorwort von Karin Liebhart
ISBN 978-3-8382-0435-2

120 *Ruslana Vovk*
Die Offenheit der ukrainischen Verfassung für das Völkerrecht und die europäische Integration
Mit einem Vorwort von Alexander Blankenagel
ISBN 978-3-8382-0481-9

121 *Mykhaylo Banakh*
Die Relevanz der Zivilgesellschaft bei den postkommunistischen Transformationsprozessen in mittel- und osteuropäischen Ländern
Das Beispiel der spät- und postsowjetischen Ukraine 1986-2009
Mit einem Vorwort von Gerhard Simon
ISBN 978-3-8382-0499-4

122 *Michael Moser*
Language Policy and the Discourse on Languages in Ukraine under President Viktor Yanukovych (25 February 2010–28 October 2012)
ISBN 978-3-8382-0497-0 (Paperback edition)
ISBN 978-3-8382-0507-6 (Hardcover edition)

ibidem-Verlag / *ibidem* Press
Melchiorstr. 15
70439 Stuttgart
Germany

ibidem@ibidem.eu
www.ibidem-verlag.com
www.ibidem.eu